IF YOU DREAM OF

Nakedness—you may fear exposure
and disgrace

Apes—beware!

Lobster—a new romance may be on the way

MONEY—you may grow poor

In this fascinating guide to the mysterious phenomenon of dreaming, Alan Levy gives a practical method for the interpretation of your most common dreams. In addition, he discusses dreams of famous people—such as Lincoln's vision of his own funeral . . . the dream that made Alexander the Great conqueror of the world . . . Freud's dreams, which guided him to an understanding of psychoanalysis—and describes the exciting research being done into the very nature of dreaming.

Whether your dreams are pleasant or terrifying, they carry messages important to you.
INTERPRET YOUR DREAMS . . . and find out what they are telling you!

SO-AYU-119

Interpret your dreams

Alan Levy

PYRAMID BOOKS ▲ NEW YORK

To MEYER and FRANCES LEVY

INTERPRET YOUR DREAMS

A PYRAMID BOOK
First printing, December 1962

PYRAMID BOOKS *are published by Pyramid Publications, Inc.,*
444 Madison Avenue, New York 22, New York, U.S.A.

Table of Contents

CHAPTER ONE:

The Democracy of Dreams

When Greek met Greek on Athenian streets one day almost five centuries before the birth of Christ, they talked about just one thing: Somebody had stolen a priceless golden goblet from the temple of the god Hercules. The authorities were baffled. The public was outraged.

That night, however, the poet Sophocles dreamed that Hercules himself appeared and identified the thief to him.

Although Sophocles was both a dreamer and an amateur detective, he was—for a while—unable to accept the evidence of dreams. He said nothing.

But he had the same dream the next night.

And the next night.

Finally, he took his "information" to the authorities.

With nothing to go on except Sophocles' dream, the Greek authorities arrested the culprit he had named and tortured the man until he confessed and led them to the stolen treasure.

The goblet was restored to the temple, which henceforth was known as the Temple of Hercules the Indicator.

Poets can dream and so can common men. Twenty-three centuries after Sophocles had solved the mystery of the golden goblet, a tinker in Swaffham, England, had a dream. "If you go to London Bridge," his dream informed him, "you will learn news of great import to you."

In the morning, the tinker told his wife of the dream. She assured him that, if he ate less for dinner, he wouldn't be bothered by foolish visions. The tinker fol-

7

lowed her advice, but he had the same dream the next night. And the next night.

"Enough, woman!" he told his wife—and he set out for London Bridge.

It took the humble tinker three days to tread the ninety miles from Swaffham to London, a city he had never visited before. London Bridge was exactly the way it had appeared in his dream—to every last detail, including the cranny before which he was supposed to wait.

The Swaffham tinker stood on London Bridge all day. Nothing happened. After three days, he was getting ready to abandon his vigil and go home when a well-dressed stranger accosted him.

"Harrumph, my good man," the stranger began. "I have been observing you. Are you waiting for anyone in particular?"

The disgruntled tinker told about his dream and the stranger chortled. When his laughter subsided, he told the tinker: "You, sir, are a confounded fool! Are you so rich that you can afford to abandon your work to wait for a dream to come true?"

"Perhaps you're right, sir," the Swaffham tinker replied sheepishly.

"Perhaps? You say perhaps!" the stranger repeated incredulously. "Let me tell you something, fellow. I myself, were I disposed to trust such things, might right now go deep into the country on just such a fool's errand as yours."

"Indeed, sir?" said the Swaffham tinker.

"For three nights this week," the pompous stranger continued, "I have dreamed that if I went to a town called Swaffham—which is, I believe, somewhere in Norfolk—and there dug under an apple tree in a garden on the north side of town, I would find a chest of money. Fortunately, *I* can ill afford to be an idler who would follow his fancies! *You* can less afford to be such a one! My good man, go back to your home—wherever it is —and work hard at your calling and you will find there the riches that you have come here so foolishly to seek."

The tinker thanked the stranger for his advice, asked him a few more questions about his dream, and hurried home to Swaffham. In the garden on the north side of town, his spade struck pay dirt. The treasure chest was there and the tinker became a country squire who thenceforth freely dispensed advice to humbler men.

From Biblical times to modern times, dreams have been a source of infinite wonderment. Joseph interpreted Pharaoh's dream of seven good ears of corn and seven thin ears as God's prophecy of seven good years followed by seven lean years. A Chinese poet once mused: "I dreamed last night that I was a butterfly and now I don't know whether I am a man who dreamed he was a butterfly or perhaps a butterfly who now dreams that he is a man." Hippocrates, the Father of Medicine, contended that dreams were the activity of the soul, which roamed free only when the body slept.

Less scholarly men shared Hippocrates' view of dreams. In Sumatra, Malaya, and India, it was once an offense to blacken or stain the face of a sleeper because this would disguise him and thereby confuse his returning soul. In the Philippines, it was a serious crime to awaken a sleeper. The natives feared that the soul might not have time to return to the body—and this, they believed, was how some people died in their sleep.

To African Zulus, the appearance of a dead ancestor in a dream means impending disaster to the whole tribe. No matter where a Zulu is, if he dreams of a dead ancestor, he must abandon everything, return to his village, and sound a warning. Even Zulus on United Nations duty are not exempt.

Nineteenth-century British justice took still another view of dreams. A sleepwalker dreamed that a wild beast was about to pounce on him. To protect himself, the sleepwalker picked up the nearest object and hurled it at the imaginary beast. His weapon happened to be a sleeping child, whose brains were unexpectedly dashed out against a wall. The remorseful sleepwalker was tried for willful murder and acquitted by a court, which defined dreams as "normal temporary insanity." (Even today, some experts believe that insanity is merely a waking dream.)

Elsewhere in the British Isles, dreams play a powerful but less treacherous role. In Wales, Midsummer Eve is considered prime time to dream. On that wondrous night, if you place a sprig of mistletoe beneath your pillow, you will have a dream that foretells the future.

In the Hebrides, if you eat a dry cake or a whole salted herring in three bites on Hallowe'en and then go off to sleep without drinking any liquids, you are promised a prophetic dream. One American dream addict, who tried this experiment recently, reported: "I dreamed I died of thirst."

Anyway, for an unmarried girl, the place to dream on Halloween is not the Hebrides, but County Leitrim in Ireland.

There—on October 31 only—she must search for a branch of briar growing in the ground and twisted backwards to form a loop with the trunk of a tree. Having found this, she must creep through its loop three times. Then she should snap off the briar branch, take it unobtrusively to her bedroom, and put it under her pillow —without telling a soul, mind you! Exhausted by her search, her acrobatics, and all this secrecy, she will then dream of her future husband.

Undoubtedly, no man thus selected would stand a dream of a chance against the will of such a doughty and determined colleen. Once she has found him, she will never let him go. After all, she might have to go through the same rigamarole again!

In America, where life is less rugged, all you have to do to conjure up the man of your dreams is put a slice of wedding cake beneath your pillow. Or, if wedding cake is not available in your community, take a walnut and a hazelnut and some nutmeg. Grate them together and mix with butter and sugar. Then roll this mixture into small pills. Take nine pills before going to bed.

Either way is effective—but the wedding-cake method is less fattening if you don't eat your cake in the morning.

Only in America have technology and hard-sell advertising successfully merchandised dreams to the masses. Here, the faithful rely on various dream interpreters to guide them in playing the numbers game and the stock market; to determine the sexes of unborn children; to tell readers whether to buy, sell, or invest . . . copulate, seduce, elope, or divorce . . . yield or resist . . . apply or resign . . . take it or leave it . . . shape up, ship out, or stay put.

Each year, Americans buy thousands of copies of *Old Aunt Dinah's Policy Player's Sure Guide to Lucky Dreams and Lucky Numbers* or the rival *Napoleon's Book of Fate Captured at the Battle of Leipsic with Interpretations of Dreams*. Many buy both—and ponder conflicting advice. For example, *Napoleon's* states that "for a young woman to dream that she is in love with and embraced by a gorilla means that she will have one of the handsomest and wisest men in the neighborhood for a suitor and will be envied by all the marriageable ladies in the district." On the other hand, *Old Aunt Dinah's* declares uncompromisingly: "To dream of apes is not good."

Perhaps in the Bronx Zoo or at Cape Canaveral or in the African bush at this moment in history, some wise old monkey is telling a disciple: "To dream of humans is not good." For science knows that apes dream. Cats dream. Sheep dream. Cows dream. Horses dream. Freely translated, a Hungarian proverb goes: "The goose dreams of corn, the pig of acorns, and the woodpecker of great oaks." Parrots and nightingales also dream. But man is the only creature who has frequently put dreams to good use—as inspiration (Joan of Arc), as ideals (the American Dream); as therapy (dream interpretation is a key to Freudian psychoanalysis).

Psychoanalytic lecturer Erich Fromm has observed: "To understand the language of dreams is an art which, like any other art, requires knowledge, talent, practice, and patience. Talent, the effort to practice what one has learned, and patience cannot be acquired by reading a book. But the knowledge necessary to understand dream language can be conveyed. . . ."

It is not a difficult or obscure language. Unlike the languages we studied in high school, it is not easy to forget—once mastered. And it is a language everyone speaks, although few of us know what we are saying.

For Dreamland is the truest Democracy of all: *Science insists that everyone dreams every time he sleeps.* Rich men dream and poor men dream; poets and Philistines; pacifists and warmongers; sane men and madmen. The man who assures you confidently that *he* never dreams doesn't know himself so well as he thinks—unless he is a full-time insomniac. Furthermore, one psychiatrist claims that insomnia can result from "a need to escape dreaming or fear of what may be expressed by the unconscious mind in dreams."

The only safely dreamless state is Death itself. Until we migrate there, each of us spends roughly a third of life in sleep—and a sixth of that time in Dreamland. In a life span of seventy years, you will devote a total of almost four years to dreaming. They need not be wasted years. In fact, they compare favorably to what four years of college can do for you:

. . . In dreams, you can learn to understand yourself, your desires, and your hidden resources.

. . . In dreams, you are stimulated to explore the world within you.

. . . In dreams, you have a rare chance to give free rein to your imagination. "We live by night and not by day," Lord Byron said.

. . . Unlike a college education, it doesn't cost you anything to dream.

. . . And, while a college education yields only as much as you put into it, a dream can reward the undeserving and torment the blessed meek.

The best summation of a dream's role was spoken in

the third century by Hesda, a Babylonian scholar who said: "A dream which is not understood is like a letter which is not opened."

CHAPTER TWO:

The Stuff of Dreams

Seventeen centuries after Hesda compared an uninterpreted dream to an unopened letter, one of America's foremost dream authorities, Dr. Calvin S. Hall, declared: "A dream is a personal document, a letter to oneself. It is not a newspaper story or a magazine article."

Does this represent 1,700 years of progress?

Science has not been slumbering between the third century and today. Over the centuries, scientists have been diligently torturing their fellow man in the name of Dream Research.

Under hypnotic suggestion, a 28-year-old nursemaid was commanded to "dream of intercourse with your father." In France an indefatigable scholar monitored the final dreams of dying hospital patients. He also rushed to scenes of tragedy in the hope of learning whether a drowning man truly re-lives his life in one last dream. In America, hard-hearted dream researchers deprived three persons of water—and all other fluids—for twenty-four hours. Just before going to sleep—perchance to dream, perchance to gasp from thirst—the victims were fed . . . *salted* . . . *peanuts!*

Other scientists deprived unfortunate dreamers not of fluids, but of dreams. Whenever an electroencephalograph showed that they were starting to dream, they were awakened. "How would this affect their daily life?" the scientists wondered.

At a school in Westfield, Massachusetts, twenty female students were each fed a crushed clove just before bedtime so that their teacher could learn if their dreams would then involve the sensation of taste.

And, over a period of several years, a British researcher tormented no fewer than 6,000 sleeping children to ascertain what they were dreaming.

The annals of man's inhumanity to man are crammed with ghastly tales of Dream Research. If it is any solace to the victims of these seemingly mad scientists, their sacrifices were not in vain. The findings that resulted from their agonies form an impressive and useful miscellany. For example:

. . . Hypnotic suggestion worked. The nursemaid who had been commanded to commit dream incest with her father had a dream jam-packed with genital symbols: *"My father handed me a big and a large key. It looked like the key to a house. When I opened the bag, a snake jumped out."*

. . . The morbid French scientist discovered that dying people dream primarily of flying. They are rising or being borne upward. Sometimes, they fight to keep from flying; one woman died clutching the iron bars of her bed for dear life. In most cases, however, they find flying a blessed relief from pain. The scientist—whose bedside manner was said to be impeccable—reported that at the very end all life seems to concentrate in dreams, while the outlying districts of the body wither and die. His subjects, incidentally, were carefully selected: some were religious and others atheistic; some were dying peacefully and others painfully.

. . . The same Frenchman debunked the myth that a drowning man's entire life passes before him. By interviewing drowning persons who were lucky enough to be rescued (or kept alive long enough to relate their dreams), he learned that a drowning man sees a particularly vivid scene from childhood followed by five or six flickering scenes from later life. These give a false impression of completeness. Since this discovery, not even drowning people have been permitted by science to possess illusions.

. . . The thirsty dreamers had a total of fifteen dreams, only three of which were related to thirst. None dreamed of salted peanuts. From tormenting these dreamers, Science also learned that men can sleep under the most adverse circumstances.

. . . The poor souls who were awakened whenever they dared to dream began to suffer in waking life from tension, anxiety, fatigue, distraction, amnesia, and clumsiness. But, thanks to them, Science verified Man's absolute need to have dreams.

. . . The twenty clove-tongued girls reported a total of 250 dreams over twenty days. Only seventeen of the dreams involved taste. Only three taste dreams were of cloves.

One of the most interesting experiments was performed on several young men of college age at Virginia Beach early in the 1950's. Known as Project X, it was performed under controlled conditions by the Association for Research and Enlightenment. Free of charge, the young men were given sweat baths, massages, sand packs, gland purifying drugs, and stimulants—in short, everything their souls could desire. They were fed together and subjected to fasting periods simultaneously. They received equal doses of physical, mental, and spiritual acitivty—including meditation periods, prayer sessions, and inspirational lectures. Life was one big Y.M.C.A. for them, but with one catch: They were required to record all their dreams.

How did the good life affect their dreams? Over a period of three weeks their dreams followed these patterns:

John (the youths' names are fictitious) dreamed of a struggle between good and evil. In the first week, his dreams were on a simple cops-and-robbers level: *"Some men were chasing me. Policemen!"* . . . *"Gangsters and policemen were fighting it out for possession of a house."* . . . *"I was a detective."* In the second week, they became more subtle: *A conflict between two Army officers who are close friends . . . A ball team turns on one of*

*its players and unites against him . . . An appearance
before a woman judge.* In the third week, his dreams
included such subtle dilemmas as *whether to return an
overdue library book or use it to maximum cultural advantage* and *how active an earnest young man ought to
be in his college fraternity.* Thanks to the good life and
regulated introspection, John had a whole new set of
problems when the experiment ended.

Freddie dreamed consistently of eating or washing
dishes in the first week. In the second week, he apparently
left the dishes for others to wash and dreamed primarily
of eating: *"Listening to a lecture on foods. Speaker
stated we don't need to eat."* . . . *"A friend of mine pur-
chased a box of Ritz crackers."* . . . *"I told a girl friend
that she should eat vegetables."* . . . *"Was with a group
swimming. After a while, they brought out a round tray
with pork sausages and pancakes."* But in the third
week, Freddie's mind had apparently emerged from the
kitchen. Ten of his fourteen recorded dreams involved
colors and aesthetics. None involved eating or dish-
washing. In his dreams, at least, he had overcome
gluttony.

Bernie's dreams had no recurring themes the first week.
In the second week, however, he dreamed of fried eggs,
meat, and his sister. In the third week, he dreamed that
Nelson Eddy was cooking liver steaks and seasoning
them with pepper. Bernie told Nelson Eddy not to pepper his. Bernie's dreams proved the least rewarding of
the experiment. They bore little relation to his spiritual
life. Perhaps he was inheriting some of Freddie's left-
over food dreams.

Herb dreamed of strawberries, ice cream, radishes,
and his fiancée in the first week. In the second week, he
dreamed of Christ and his fiancée. In the third week,
he dreamed of some of the boys participating in Project
X with him.

Hank dreamed in the first week of liver-and-onions,
peanut-butter-and-jelly, and a battle of wits with
Groucho Marx in a library. By the third week, however,
he was dreaming the text of a book that he had never

read. The Project X people˜then decided that Hank had just had a clairvoyant experience.

Fascinating as its findings were, Project X's conclusions proved rather anticlimactic. From all their important research, the Project X people merely decided: "The personality of sleep maintains the fundamental connection between the organism and the spiritual world." But it is hard to think of Nelson Eddy and Groucho Marx as missing links.

In all fairness to embattled dream researchers, not all of them are guilty of sadism or incompleteness. Some of the more noble scientists have, in fact, tortured *themselves* to ascertain small details. In 1878, Alfred Maury had a drop of eau de Cologne placed on his nose while he slept. He dreamed that he was shopping for perfume in Cairo. And, in another experiment, A. J. Cubberley, a psychologist, pasted tiny squares of gummed paper on various parts of his body to create tension and skin sensations when he slept. On a night when he put the paper on the soles of his feet, he dreamed of dancing in the dark like a veritable Fred Astaire. With paper on his chest, he dreamed of a doctor applying a stethoscope. With paper on the upper part of his back, he dreamed he was bending over backward to catch a glimpse of an airplane flying overhead.

Some scientists—instead of torturing human guinea pigs—have merely intruded on sufferers in the line of duty. A French doctor, treating an unfortunate woman who had lost part of her skull, observed that her brain bulged when she dreamed. In dreamless sleep, her brain appeared motionless to the naked eye. Another French doctor reported the case of a dark-haired man who had a nightmare and—*sacre bleu!*—his hair turned completely white. Nightmares have even killed people— by raising a dreamer's blood pressure and causing hemorrhage.

Scientists have stumbled upon the dreams of pregnant women, schizophrenics, lion tamers, transvestites, and paraplegics. Epileptics, they say, dream of flying and falling. Drug addicts have always fascinated the dream researchers. Hashish, they say, has been known to affect the speed of dreaming and even induce homicidal mania. Thus the word *assassin* is derived from the word *hashish*.

Alcoholics have actually badgered the scientists with their dreams, so there is no shortage of material on this substantial segment of our population. Drunkards, it turns out, dream of rats, reptiles, and vermin far more than they dream of pink elephants.

Dreams, incidentally, afford confirmation of the Alcoholics Anonymous theory that alcoholism is never cured, just arrested. Reformed alcoholics have reported that after several years the physical craving may vanish from waking life and even be replaced by an aversion to liquor, but they still have dreams of drinking liquor, craving liquor, and enjoying liquor. At an earlier stage of rehabilitation, dreams can also be useful, according to a psychoanalyst who noted: "With patients who have been subject to alcoholic excess, I have found that when they *dream* of drunkeness instead of actually becoming drunk, they have reached a stage where the mental causes of the habit are becoming accessible and therefore hopeful of solution."

The scientists have also compiled a vast library on what people *don't* dream. One report reads: "Businessmen ordinarily do not dream about their business affairs, factory workers do not dream about their jobs, artists do not dream about paintings, students do not dream about studying, and housewives do not dream about household activities." As for the people who claim they never dream, Science has pounced on them and unmasked them as dreamers with bad memories and so many repressions that they never allow their dreams to emerge into their conscious minds.

One caste-conscious French woman doctor screened thirty-seven dreamers according to jobs and education. After five years, she reported that people who are educated and mentally active dream more often than others. Her *elite* also dreamed more varyingly and with greater complexity than her uneducated patients, whose dreams were often mere reproductions of waking experience. Her eggheads (attorneys, journalists, chemists, teachers, etc.) reported only three to ten nights a month when they could recall no dreams at all. Her workmen, however, reported twice as many "dreamless nights." To her, this proved conclusively that lawyers were smarter than laborers, but modern scientists later noted that, at best, it meant that lawyers were more disciplined thinkers.

British scientists have converged with particular glee on the dreams of blind, deaf, and dumb people. If their studies are to be believed, the blind generally dream in terms of hearing, touch, and smell. Those who were born with sight but lost it later in life occasionally see in their dreams. Deaf people who once had the gift of hearing can still discern sounds within their dreams, but the congenitally deaf often have dreams in which people express themselves in sign language or on paper. Deaf people often dream of being the first to sound an alarm. The blind have recurring nightmares of being trapped in fires or air raids.

On the other side of the ocean but in the same dream area, Helen Keller—blind and deaf—has written:

"In my dreams I have sensations, odors, tastes, and ideas which I do not remember to have had in reality. Perhaps they are the glimpses which my mind catches through the veil of sleep of my earliest babyhood. I have heard 'the trampling of many waters.' Sometimes a wonderful light visits me in sleep. . . . I gaze and gaze until it vanishes. I smell and taste much as in my waking hours, but the sense of touch plays a less important part. In sleep I almost never grope. No one guides me. Even in a crowded street, I am self-sufficient and I enjoy an independence quite foreign to my physical life. . . . I am delighted to be thus endowed, if only in sleep."

Under normal circumstances, an infant is not endowed with dreams until he is somewhere between the ages of three months and six months. In their very early years, children have a problem distinguishing between dreams and real events—partly because children don't know any better; partly because these dreams tend to be literal re-creations of the previous day's experiences. If such dreams have a few impressionistic touches, they then seem more vivid and real than life itself. Take a case not unknown to dream researchers or newspaper readers: A child dreams of killing a parent . . . awakens to find the parent dead (usually of natural causes) . . . and then confesses to murder. In almost every case, it is safe to ignore a confession of murder if the suspect is under the age of five.

Even at the age of five, some children retain their innocence. According to the Briton who woke up 6,000 children and collected their dreams, 15 per cent of the dreams by five-year-olds involved Santa Claus and re-lated matters (for example, gifts). But innocence van-ishes quickly—to be replaced by fear, guilt, anxiety, and hostility. By the age of seven, children dream more of burglars and prowlers.

Among the dreams of children in the five-to-seven-year-old bracket are these samples:

"*I dreamed that a tiger came into our house and ate Mommy and Daddy and my brother and me and then I woke up and said: 'It isn't true!'*"

A boy who had broken a cup during the day and con-cealed his crime dreamed that a burglar entered the house, took nothing, but broke all the cups.

Another boy who professed to adore his baby sister fooled nobody when he reported this dream: "*A thief came, took our white baby, and left a black one instead.*"

A sophisticated seven-year-old dreamed: "*I went to my auntie's and she gave me some biscuits. We had a tea party. Then a soldier on crutches came along and said, 'Hey, Auntie! Let's waltz!'*"

The demon researcher of children's dreams, Mr. C. W. Kimmins, noted that five-to-seveners in low-rent dis-tricts dreamed more about toys than well-to-do children did. But the underprivileged children in this age group dreamed less about food than their older brothers and sisters. Why? If a family is starving, its little ones are generally the last to feel the pinch.

Between the ages of eight and fourteen, young dreamers learn much about fear. Boys have a few more nightmares than girls. The boys now fear burglars, lions, tigers, and bulls. The girls fear strangers, dogs, rats, mice, and snakes. Both sexes dream fearfully of older people. Around the age of ten, dreams of falling begin to bother boys and girls. As girls approach puberty, they dream about religion, angels, and heaven. At fourteen, their dreams begin to involve jealousy of other females. Boys are slower in attaining this level.

Among the dreams of children in the eight-to-fourteen age bracket are these:

An eight-year-old boy: *"I dreamed that I was put in a washing machine. Then I was wrung out in a mangle and hung out on a line to dry. But it began to rain. My mother took me inside and ironed me. The iron was hot, so I woke up."*

A fourteen-year-old girl: *"I was touring Germany with my friend Rachel and we went around asking people if they spoke English. If they said yes, we told them to hold up their hands. Then we shot them. I dreamed that we killed every English-speaking German in Germany."*

A twelve-year-old boy: *"I was being pursued by cartons of Jello. As they got near me, the Jello—in all different colors and flavors—came out of the packages. Each blob of Jello had a wooden fork. The blobs of Jello each tried to stick their forks into me. They made growling noises and I woke up. . . ."*

Between the ages of fourteen and sixteen, adolescents dream of dying—girls from natural causes, boys heroically. Teachers will be happy to hear that, in this age bracket, both sexes dream of school more often than at any other time. One sixteen-year-old girl is afflicted by talking books: *Her history book asks her, "Are you, perchance, Grover Cleveland?" Her geography book inquires: "Where were you born and what is its principal product?" Her English textbook gives her a withering stare and intones: "Winston tastes good AS a cigarette should."*

By the age of sixteen, adolescents are also dreaming—with varying degrees of enthusiasm—about sex. Most young men have begun to experience "wet dreams" approximately once a month. These nocturnal expressions of sexual energy are looked upon with distress and some shame by their originators. Although "wet dreams" do pose problems—usually involving bed linens and pajamas—they should be contemplated with pride. In the hypocritical waking world, after all, various arbitrary standards exist to determine adulthood: You are a man when you lose your virginity, become Bar Mitzvahed or confirmed, are graduated from high school, learn to drive, or are served beer in a tavern. But in the dream world, you may consider yourself an adult dreamer when you have your first "wet dream."

This is not an anti-feminist standard. Contrary to popular belief, women also have wet dreams. The Kinsey Report on *Sexual Behavior in the Human Female* demonstrated this conclusively. Female wet dreams tend to be more imaginative than those of men. They frequently go beyond the dreamer's actual experience. Thus, if a maiden reports a wet dream orgasm, her fiancé need not doubt her virginity.

As a matter of fact, female wet dreams are good omens—even in thirty-five-year-old virgins. Kinsey contended that wet dreams are a good measure of a woman's intrinsic sexuality and her sexual capacities.

Wet or dry, a dream itself usually lasts about as long as the selected shorts at a single-feature movie house— ten to thirty minutes. On the average, the typical adult dreamer has one dream every ninety minutes. Dreams tend to get longer as the night wears on. In eight hours of sleep, you are likely to have six dreams—of which the third or fourth will be the most vivid. It is certainly the one you will have the best chance of remembering later.

In the usual eight hours of sleep, your dreams are likely to travel full circle. Your first dream will probably start with reasonably current events—for example, the previous day's doings. The subsequent dreams will delve deeper and deeper into your past, but as your night's rest nears an end, your dreams will return to the present.

Time within dreams, however, can be eccentric. C. W. Leadbeater, a noted theosophist, has recorded the case of a patient who fell asleep in a dentist's chair while two of his teeth were being extracted. The patient happened to be a college professor. *He dreamed of giving numerous lectures—in their painful entirety. He also dreamed of giving a special and particularly verbose lecture before the Royal Society. He was midway through his special lecture when someone in the audience annoyed him by saying, "It's all over now!" The pompous professor tried to ignore this interruption and rambled on, but then the same voice said, "They are both out."* The professor awoke to find himself in the dentist's chair. He had been asleep for less than two minutes.

What else do we know about dreams? Various scientists—including some of the tormentors I mentioned earlier—have helped to complete this profile:

Color: Approximately two out of three dreams are in black-and-white. A few people dream entirely in color. Some people never dream in color. Most of us dream in color every now and then. "Color in dreams," said Dr. Calvin S. Hall, "yields no information about the personality of the dreamer."

Taste: Professor W. S. Monroe, who put cloves on the tongues of twenty girl dreamers, also found that—with or without any help from him—taste sensations occur very rarely in dreams.

Movement: Working on fifty-five females at Westfield Normal School, Professor Monroe found action (such as flying and falling) in five per cent of their dreams. But, in other studies, as many as thirty-three per cent of the dreams were active. Men have more active dreams than women.

Sight, Sound and Smell: Still putting the girls at Westfield Normal School through their paces at night, Professor Monroe learned that 67 per cent of their dreams involved seeing, 26 per cent hearing, and one per cent smelling.

Personnel: The dreamer almost always plays a role in his or her dream. One dream out of six is a solo—with the dreamer as the only character. The average cast is three. More than half the characters in dreams are recognizable to the dreamer. They are primarily family members, close friends, mistresses, secretaries, bosses, and others with whom the dreamer is emotionally involved.

Setting: Most dreams take place indoors—in homes, kitchens, bedrooms, cars, public transportation, and jails. No more than twenty per cent take place in the wide open spaces or on the ocean. About five per cent take place nowhere in particular.

For thousands of years, practical men have been trying to put dreams in their place. Do they originate inside or outside the human body? Plato decided that dreams and insanity came from the liver; serious thinking from the head. Sir Thomas Browne, a seventeenth century British physician, blamed many dreams on unbalanced diets. "Some food makes us turbulent, some gives quiet dreams," he declared in a ramble through history. "Cato, who doted upon cabbage, might find the cruel effects thereof in his sleep. . . . Egyptians might find some advantage by their superstitious abstinence from onions. Pythagoras might have had calmer sleeps if he had totally abstained from beans." The question then arises: *If Pythagoras had had calmer sleeps, would he have been able to keep millions of geometry students awake pondering the intricacies of the Pythagorean Theorem* $(a^2 + b^2 = c^2)$?

Other authorities have attributed dreams to such internal stimulation as thirst, undigested pickles mixed with ice cream, acid indigestion, and nervous stomach. A whole school of thought is dedicated to proving conclusively that dreams of flying come from the upward and downward motion of the lobes of the lungs. It is best to skim over such small-bore research as quickly as possible.

But those who believe in general that dreams have a visceral origin will find solace in these two stories from the annals of dream research:

There was a suburban housewife who used to dream of murder every time she ate pheasant.

One night, after a hearty pheasant dinner, she dreamed that her husband summoned her and said: "Now, Bess, please don't scream or make a fuss. I must tell you something you won't like to hear. I have to kill a man. It's necessary. He's in terrible pain."

Her husband then ushered her into his den, where a young man lay writhing on the floor. A dagger was stuck in his chest.

"I see what you mean," the wife said alertly. "We must dispose of him at once. But how?"

"Leave that to me," her husband replied efficiently. The wife turned away. The husband bent over the young man, who made a gurgling sound and then subsided forever.

"That's that," her husband remarked as he wiped blood off his hands. "Now to get rid of the body. I want you to send for Mr. Malatesta's moving van and tell him I would like to drive it myself."

When Mr. Malatesta had delivered his van to the door, the wife returned to the den. Her husband was struggling with the corpse. "Darling," he said, "can I trouble you for three of those giant-sized shopping bags that you bring home from the shopping center? And your carving knife?"

His wife obliged. Working together, they cut the body into three parts and packaged it neatly. Then they set off with their bloody cargo in the moving van. They left the three paper bags in the freezer of an abandoned pizzeria.

All went well until they returned the moving van. Mr. Malatesta complained: "There is blood in my padded wagon."

"Nonsense!" the husband said glibly. "That's just paint."

Mr. Malatesta began to sob.

"I'll shut his mouth forever," the husband murmured to his wife, who screamed. Mr. Malatesta called the police. The body was discovered in the pizzeria. In jail, husband and wife argued over who would go to the gallows first. The husband offered to shut her mouth forever.

It is safe to say that this particular dreamer should avoid eating pheasant. When she eats pheasant *under glass,* her subsequent dreams are unspeakable. But she insists that she cannot give up eating pheasant.

The other visceral dream comes from the files of Mr. Havelock Ellis, the British psychologist and author, who reports only its effect, not its content:

"A young woman was impelled by a distended bladder, while still asleep, to get out of bed and proceed to carry out the suggested action, but without further precautions, on the floor. She was only awakened by an exclamation from her sister, who had been aroused by the sound."

The embarrassing result was clear—if untidy—evidence that her dream had a physical origin, according to Ellis.

There are also scientists who try to find external origins for dreams. They have an impressive file of case histories:

A man who fell asleep while wearing a tight shirt dreamed he was hanged.

A spinster who slept with a hot-water bottle dreamed that Mount Vesuvius was erupting.

A man stuck by a pin in his sleep dreamed of being stabbed in a duel.

A child who was having a bad dream was pinched by his brother. The child then dreamed that a lobster clawed him.

Sleepers who burrow under blankets dream of being buried alive.

An old Yankee whose nightcap came off dreamed that Indians were scalping him.

The most famous instance of all involved Alfred Maury, a distinguished French scientist who was afflicted by faulty furniture. One night, the rail at the head of his bed came off and landed gently upon Maury's neck. *Instantly, he dreamed that he was living in the Reign of Terror, where Robespierre and other leftists sentenced him to death. In his dream, Maury climbed the scaffold, was tied to a board, and then was guillotined. He felt his head part from his body before he woke up intact.*

The sun plays a key role in most theories that dreams originate outside the body. One case history notes: "A certain Scherner fell asleep one morning, with the sun shining directly in his eyes and he had a dream of a fiery dragon approaching him. The dragon came on faster and faster and then slower and slower, at last stopping dead and making off again. Scherner woke up to find that a heavy cloud was just passing over the sun."

Havelock Ellis tells of a man who once fell asleep in a theatre during one of the last scenes of *Cavalleria Rusticana*. As the tenor's voice rose, the sleeping operagoer dreamed that the tenor was climbing stairs and ladders.

Smog and other brands of air pollution have been blamed for the high incidence of nightmares in big cities. One expert also asserts: "The fumes of carbon bisulphide impregnating the atmosphere of rubber factories induce dreams in which the sleeper leaps over precipices or is brutally murdered." Thus, lucrative jobs in rubber plants may possess hidden dissuaders.

Nightmares and daydreams, incidentally, are two of the more controversial aspects of dream science. Definitive research on nightmares grows more urgent each year: Latest statistics show that unpleasant dreams outnumber pleasant ones by three to one. My own nightmares usually occur early in slumber, which lends credence to my favorite theory: *A nightmare is an expression of the dreamer's fear of death.* Going to sleep at night is very much like going to sleep forever.

The word *nightmare* derives from another theory: Ancient Britons and Romans attributed bad dreams to a huge female horse which, they said, camped out at night on sleepers' bosoms and caused a feeling akin to suffocation.

Daydreams, on the other hand, are harmless—so long as the dreamer isn't behind the wheel of a car! Although some consider daydreams mere reminiscences, I see them as a preview of coming attractions—the night dreams we may have when we go to sleep. Most daydreamers are able to yank themselves back to waking life quite readily; in fact, their daydreams sometimes are the fantasies that make waking life tolerable. Another theory has labeled the daydream an intrusion of night dreaming upon daily activity. Still others find external causes for daydreaming; this is known as the Walter Mitty school of thought.

Havelock Ellis, however, has refuted all theories about external origins of dreams with these words: "The ray of sunlight that falls on the dreamer, the falling off of his bedclothes, the indigestible supper he ate last night—these can no more 'account' for his dream than the postman's knock can account for the contents of the letter he delivers."

Although scientists always seem to end up comparing dreams to letters—opened or unopened, special delivery or postage due, certified or fourth class—another analogy also is valid: *Dreams are night watchmen who protect our sleep from interruption.* An entire category— Dreams of Convenience—has mystified and delighted Organized Science through the ages. Let me cite a few:

. . . The first is all my own: *I am dreaming happily of seducing Miss Susan Strasberg when a tire backfires outside my window. Do I panic? No. Do I awaken? No. In my dream, I am simply called to war, thrown into a trench, exposed to a barrage of gunfire, captured, thrown into Stalag 17, repatriated, freed, and hired by Sears Roebuck as an interior decorator.* True, I have lost Miss Susan Strasberg forever, but the important thing is that I have slept on and on. The tire explosion has been worked into my dream as a war scene.

. . . Mungo Park was not a place. He was a man—an explorer. On a journey through Africa, Mr. Mungo Park needed both rest and water. The latter was not readily available, but when he slept he dreamed of green hills and valleys. Thus, he managed to sleep despite his thirst. But when he awoke he was as parched as ever.

. . . *"It shall even be as when an hungry man dreameth, and, behold, he eateth; but he awaketh, and his soul is empty; or as when a thirsty man dreameth, and, behold, he drinketh; but he awaketh, and, behold, he is faint."*—Isaiah, xxix, 8. Arctic and Antarctic explorers frequently dream of receiving all the mail, females and steam heat that their shivering hearts could desire. If they are in distress, they may dream of nuclear submarines hurtling to their rescue. If they are hungry, they may dream of eating their faithful Huskies. Such dreams enable them to face the arduous day ahead at full strength.

Unemployment counselors are familiar with former job holders who, when their alarm clocks rang on weekdays, would dream that it was Sunday—and go right on sleeping.

. . . In a town not far from Horse Cave, Kentucky, a social climber dreamed that her mother had disappeared. In her dream, she was forbidden to look for her. Upon awakening, the dreamer was so troubled that she began commuting to Louisville, where she saw a psychiatrist four times a week for three years. Eventually, the truth emerged: The dreamer had been born on the wrong side of the tracks, but she had married one of the wealthiest citizens of the Horse Cave area. She threw grandiose parties that earned her the reputation of "The Perle Mesta of the Horse Cave area." But her mother continued to dwell in the ancestral hovel on the wrong side of the tracks. "You have had a Dream of Convenience," the Louisville doctor assured her. "You have found the proper way to remove the stigma of your mother's address. You dispose of her in your dreams and thus you can rest easy. This is healthy. You need never have sought psychiatric help in the first place." Perhaps the doctor was underrating himself.

. . . Not far away, a Murfreesboro, Tennessee, woman actually did lose her mother. In this case, grief almost overcame her. For many months, she would awaken in the middle of the night and cry out, "Mummie! Mummie!" Since the mourner was 52, this was unhealthy. But after a few more months she began to dream of her mother. "What are you doing here, Mummie? You're dead, you know," the bereaved daughter would say. "That's what everyone thinks," her mother would reply in the dream, "but I just feigned death so I could count the number of people who would actually come to my funeral." She would then regale her daughter with tales of how she had fooled the embalmer. The daughter would have eight good hours of sleep before awakening from this miraculous Dream of Convenience. Then she would remember that her mother had been cremated.

. . . Bernard Krisher, who dwelt in a ground-floor apartment on Jane Street in Manhattan, dreamed that he was being clawed by a tiger. Since tigers seldom roam the streets of Greenwich Village, Mr. Krisher immediately invented a white hunter named Gentleman Jim Corbett, who killed the tiger. Thanks to his Dream of Convenience, Mr. Krisher fulfilled his daily quota of ten hours' sleep. But, when he awoke, he found claw marks on his bare chest. Sleeping beside him was a stray cat that had apparently leaped in through his open window during the night. Mr. Krisher kept the cat and named her Nekko.

Dreams, in general, are far more than merely convenient: they are essential. People have, quite literally, *found themselves* in dreams. Some authorities see dreams as man's only salvation. "Our memories," said the French philosopher, Henri Bergson, "are packed away under pressures like steam in a boiler. The dream is their escape valve." In daily life, a great many impressions and perceptions seem to bounce off us while we absorb the "important" ideas that seem vital to us. But these "important" ideas don't always prove so meaningful as they appeared. The insignificant thought—dismissed with a shrug—often gives us a second chance, saves a life, or changes history.

Dreams are the storehouse of these thoughts. And, even if one of these stray thoughts is every bit as unimportant as it seems, it often finds several partners in the dream life. Together, these rejects may go on to solve a problem of ours. As Carl Gustav Jung, the great psychologist, has said:

"When we lose our way among the endless details and detached events of the superficial world, what would be more natural to expect than to knock on the door of our dreams and ask for views on those problems which could reorient us toward fundamental human facts."

Another authority says: "If it were not for dreams we would be unable to live." In dreams we can tell off the boss, rob the A & P, and spit at society without paying the price. Each day in this hectic world provides us with our share of rebuffs, missed opportunities, regrets, hostilities, and aspirations. If we obeyed some of our impulses, they might prove suicidal or homicidal. But dreams enable us to enact these fantasies in privacy. They provide each one of us with the opportunity to go quietly and safely insane every night. In this manner, we can adjust to the madness of everyday life and keep our repressions from overwhelming us.

Today, all this sounds elementary and noncontroversial. But, less than a hundred years ago, the dream experts would have disputed most or all of these theories.

Then, around the turn of the century in old Vienna, Dr. Sigmund Freud discovered Man's Unconscious. He compared it to "a wild beast caged in the heart of a city."

CHAPTER THREE:

Dream Along With Freud

Sigmund Freud had six children of his own. He also had several thousand disciples. His children turned out fine: Anna, the youngest, became a famous psychoanalyst in her own right. Thanks, however, to the pomposity and lint-picking of so many of his disciples, Freud today is regarded by many laymen as either the God of an austere cult or a running joke. He was neither.

It goes without saying that Freud was a brilliant man. But he was also genial, humorous, and quite down to earth—which is more than can be said for most dream interpreters. He was born to Jewish parents in Moravia in 1856, but he lived in Vienna from the age of four until he was eighty-two. He began his university career as a student of chemistry. When he showed little aptitude for chemistry, he switched to physiology, anatomy, and then medicine. There was no psychoanalysis until Freud paved the way.

Then, as now, there were many who scoffed at Freud's findings and many more who were appalled by the truths he unearthed. There was so much animosity toward Freud, in fact, that he never was promoted to a full professorship at the University of Vienna.

Anyone who is deeply interested in dreams should read Freud's masterpiece, *The Interpretation of Dreams,* which is available inexpensively. It is now a standard psychology text. Not only does it shed light on dreams, but it also sheds light on Freud himself. It reveals, among other things, a man with a sly sense of humor and a penchant for the outrageous pun. For example:

34

The Dream: *My uncle gives me a kiss in his car.*
The Analysis: Auto-erotism.

The Dream: *On a certain road, I see a girl dressed in white and bathed in a white light.*
The Analysis: It was on this road that my love affair with a Miss White began.

The Dream: *My former governess appears in a dress of black lustre. The dress fits closely over her buttocks.*
The Analysis: My former governess was lustful.

The Dream: *I misspell Ethel's name as "Ethyl."*
The Analysis: Ethel drinks too much. If she doesn't watch out, she'll become an alcoholic.

Most of us, Freud discovered, pun in our dreams. Why? Because many puns occur to us—or start to occur—during our daily waking life. We repress them, however, because a pun—like a belch—just is not socially acceptable. It is a second-class citizen in the world of humor.

The pun's revenge is in the dream, where it is given full expression. If you deplore puns, the only way you can keep them out of your dreams is by punning in waking life. You may lose all your friends, but you'll enjoy your sleep more.

If Freud's contribution to dream research had been no more than merely recognizing the role of the pun, he would have accomplished more than many of his colleagues and rivals. But he explored our dreams far more deeply and he put them to good use in psychoanalysis.

Most Freudians of today tend to reject less psychiatrically-oriented dream books like this laymen's guide or, in particular, such hokey efforts as *Old Aunt Dinah's Dream Book* and *Anna Eva Fay's Somnolency and Guide to Dreams*. But Freud himself took a far more tolerant attitude. Long after he had become recognized as *the* authority, he wrote:

"One day I discovered to my great astonishment that the view of dreams which came nearest to the truth was not the medical but the popular one, half-involved though it still was in superstition."

What Freud accomplished was to explain scientifically why our dreams mean what we half-instinctively guessed them to mean. And, since Freud was so tolerant of the popular dream book, I would like to return a fraction of the favor by explaining Freud—as he appears to *me*. Perhaps then he can be more meaningful to *you*.

Each one of us (Freud said) contains an unknown being within himself. This stranger is the Unconscious. Your Unconscious has primitive urges, childlike habits, and often loathsome yearnings like the wish to kill somebody he loves. If you met your Unconscious on the street, you probably wouldn't recognize him. You certainly wouldn't like him. And very little of what he was saying would seem to have any bearing on you.

But, like it or not, this Unconscious is the real You —the You who was abandoned in childhood after rebuffs and disappointments. You wanted all the salt-water taffy in Coney Island, but your parents, your stomach, and financial pressures vetoed the idea. You wanted to bite off your sister's ear, but she needed it. Or, if you were a little girl, perhaps you wanted something your brother had that you didn't. . . .

You learned soon enough that you could get a reasonable amount of candy by asking for it at the proper time and saying "please." You learned that you couldn't bite off your sister's ear, but you could nibble at it affectionately. And, if you were a girl, you learned that you could probably never be a boy or a man. Maybe a career girl. Maybe a leader of men. Or, maybe when you grew up, you could have a man. But that was all.

Still, you wished.

At this point in childhood, there began to be two You's. The rational You confronted each day with a growing understanding of and respect for the rules of the game. But the real You—your Unconscious—kept on wishing. And so, like most childhood friends, the two You's grew further apart.

Just because one loses track of a childhood friend, however, he doesn't cease to exist. The rational, maturing You continued to grow in waking life. But your Unconscious dwelled in the dream life. His influence upon you was subtle. He has had—and still has—a great deal to do with your attitudes. If you ever fell in love "at first sight" with someone, you can blame it on your Unconscious. He probably had something to do with your choice or rejection of a potential marriage partner. He undoubtedly had everything to do with those snap judgments you sometimes made about a business associate or a stranger whom you hardly knew: "I just don't like him."

Every night, when you go to bed, your Unconscious finds allies. He joins up with your incomplete thoughts, unsolved problems, and seemingly rejected impressions of the preceding day. Often, your Unconscious takes the form of a recurring dream whose nightly variations are triggered by each day's events.

As an example, Freud cited the dreams of a man of thirty, who would see a yellow lion in a variety of situations. The dreamer was mystified for many years until, as Freud reported: "The young man . . . learned from his mother that [a miniature] lion had been his favorite toy in early childhood, a fact which he himself could no longer remember."

Most dreams, however, are not solved that easily— for your childhood friend, the Unconscious, assumes many disguises.

Over the years, he has become energetic, shrewd, opportunistic, and rather clever, but he remains as childish as he was when he and you first parted company.

He has reason to behave the way he does, for there are many forces out to suppress him—including you, in whose mind he dwells. He lives as deviously as a spy or a journalist in a totalitarian country. Freud has made this comparison:

"The political writer who has unpleasant truths to

tell to those in power finds himself in a like position. If he tells everything without reserve, the Government will suppress them—retrospectively in the case of a verbal expression of opinion, preventively if they are to be published in the Press.

"The writer stands in fear of the censorship; he therefore moderates and disguises the expression of his opinions. He finds himself compelled, in accordance with the sensibilities of the censor, either to refrain altogether from certain forms of attack, or to express himself in allusions instead of by direct assertions; or he must conceal his objectionable statement in an apparently innocent disguise.

"He may, for instance, tell of a contretemps between two Chinese mandarins while he really has in mind the officials of his own country. The stricter the domination of the censorship, the more thorough becomes the disguise, and, often enough, the more ingenious the means employed to put the reader on the track of the actual meaning."

Dreams express the wishes of your Unconscious. The dream is his best means to fulfill his wish, enact his fantasies, and relieve the pains of his bondage to you. Wishes vary from person to person—and so do dreams. But the man who wrote "A Dream is a Wish Your Heart Makes" came closer to the truth than he knew. Somewhere within you, your childhood friend, the Unconscious, is wishing.

The only universal wish is the urge to sleep. Sooner or later, it is gratified. Each completed dream represents, if nothing else, fulfillment of this wish. This is why dream deprivation can be as debilitating as sleep deprivation.

Because he is operating in hostile territory, your Unconscious takes a security measure that is as essential as the spy's cloak-and-dagger or the journalist's anonymity: He *condenses* his messages as ruthlessly as the *Reader's Digest*. Sometimes, he crams six or eight different wishes into one composite picture. He is, after all, on borrowed time.

Here is a contemporary example of how he works:

Let us suppose you are a suburban bachelor. If you dream that you see Cleopatra burning at a stake, you may really be wishing to:
1. Hold a barbecue.
2. Atone for having contributed to a political witch-hunt.
3. Mate with Elizabeth Taylor.
4. Read Shakespeare.
5. Give up smoking.
6. Go on sleeping.
And that is just scraping the surface of your dream.

But condensation is not enough, for the censors of your dreams might disapprove of Elizabeth Taylor because she gave money to the wrong causes. And so your Unconscious disguises his message further.

"Let's see," he muses, "Elizabeth Taylor is bad. But Shakespeare is good. So if I put a beard on Cleopatra, they'll think I'm loyal to Shakespeare."

He then anticipates other objections: "The Government approves of smoking; without the cigarette industry, the economy would topple. So I can't give up smoking. Instead, I'll double my smoking. As for witch-hunts, they're not fashionable this year. Firing squads are the big things."

Thanks to logic like this, the original composite picture is *displaced* by a scene showing a bearded Cleopatra smoking two Fatimas simultaneously while a firing squad executes her.

Your Unconscious still knows, however, that he isn't home free. His experience tells him that news censors won't tolerate such a story. Worse yet, they might even see what he's getting at.

But perhaps it doesn't have to be submitted to the news censors! The ones who censor musical comedies are much more easygoing—a bunch of tired businessmen holding down soft Government jobs.

Having condensed and displaced, your Unconscious now begins to *dramatize*. Cleopatra must become someone more universal. How about The Girl Next Door who will just happen to have a beard? That could slip by. She is loved from afar by a beardless youth—who happens to be a member of the local Volunteer Firing Squad. To work in a few romping outdoor ballets let's change the setting from an execution to a Fourth of July picnic. And, for visual effects, why not costume half the picnickers in formal garb and the others in the nude? The hero and Cleopatra—now called Patsy—both happen to be in the latter category. The folks in evening dress, looking very stern and parental, tend to disapprove of them. But one can also detect a trace of envy. . . .

Your Unconscious now has a good, commercial, seemingly uncontroversial plot about a Naked Boy Who Belongs to the Volunteer Firing Squad in love with a Naked Bearded Girl Next Door despite their villainous, well-dressed Parents.

Like all shows, it needs revisions. Like most shows, it will get revisions if it is to be worth remembering at all. But this will come *after* you wake up and try to remember it. How you tell your dream to yourself or others is exceedingly significant. This reconstruction, with all its additions and deletions, is what Freud called *secondary elaboration*.

That morning, you may tell your roommate: "I had the damnedest dream last night. I was in love with Patsy, the girl next door, and she and I went on a picnic, where we both took off our clothes. And the funny thing was: I could swear she had a mustache. . . ."

Your roommate may remind you that the girl next door is named Amy and she's only eight years old. He may also say that he's been thinking about moving elsewhere at the end of the month. . . .

Freud found Dreams of Convenience among the simplest and most undisguised forms of wish-fulfillment. "There is, for example, a dream which I can evoke as often as I please, experimentally as it were," he confessed. "If, in the evening, I eat anchovies, olives, or other strongly salted foods, I am thirsty at night and, therefore, I wake. *The waking, however, is preceded by a dream, which has always the same content, namely, that I am drinking. I am drinking long draughts of water; it tastes as delicious as only a cool drink can taste when one's throat is parched; and then I wake and find that I have an actual desire to drink.* The cause of this dream is thirst, which I perceive when I wake. From this sensation arises the wish to drink, and the dream shows me this wish as fulfilled. It thereby serves a function, the nature of which I soon surmise. I sleep well and am not accustomed to being waked by a bodily need. If I succeed in appeasing my thirst by means of the dream that I am drinking, I need not wake up in order to satisfy that thirst."

Unfortunately for Freud, this Dream of Convenience prolonged his sleep by only a few moments. He did not sleep on, for—as he so aptly put it—"the need of water to quench the thirst cannot be satisfied by a dream." (As we have seen, the explorer Mungo Park put a similar dream to better use.)

Freud also told of a young medical student named Pepi who left strict instructions with his Viennese landlady to get him up no matter how much resistance he offered.

One morning, the woman called into his room: "Herr Pepi, *achtung! achtung!* You must get up and go to the hospital. *Schnell!*"

Instantly, Pepi dreamed that he was in a hospital bed, at the foot of which a chart read: "Pepi. Medical student. Age: 22."

Pepi turned over in bed and said to himself, "If I am already at the hospital, I don't have to go there." It made such good sense that he went back to sleep.

Freud's story does not merely illuminate Dreams of Convenience. It also explains why doctors keep us waiting—and reading last week's *TV Guide*—in overcrowded anterooms.

Freud was particularly interested in the forgetting of dreams. You don't remember many of them because they are too dangerous. Even *after* you awaken, your censors are still at work. Sometimes, they settle for secondary elaboration or revisions. At other times, they suppress completely.

A dreamer had to watch his vocabulary when he told Freud a dream, for the good doctor found clues everywhere. Once, a young man—who was struggling to recall a dream of women undressing—told Freud innocently: "There are some gaps in the dream. Something is missing."

What did Freud make of these words? A great deal. Said Freud:

"The *'gaps'* are the genital apertures of the women. . . . *'Something is missing'* describes the principal characteristic of the female genitals. In his young days he burned with curiosity to see the female genitals, and was still inclined to adhere to the infantile sexual theory which attributes a male organ to women."

Breaking down all the barriers (including verbal blocks, memory lapses and repression)—and regaining contact with your childhood friend, the Unconscious—is the essence of Freudian psychoanalysis.

By exploring your dreams and identifying the prevailing unconscious desires behind them, you—with psychoanalytic help—can check the impulses that are undermining you.

You have to know *who* your enemy is before you can fight him. You can never wipe out your childhood friend, the Unconscious, but you can bring him into line. If you do, you will be able to function efficiently, perhaps happily.

If, for example, you are crippled by headaches that have no physical origin, you may learn that you are troubled because you want to see your father, who has been dead for ten years.

Does it help to know this? Yes, because you can then tell yourself that, under most circumstances, you just can't see dead people after they've been interred. And, once you have coped with the situation realistically, you have taken a step forward.

Nervous breakdowns occur when the dreamer's censors go on vacation—often because of overwork or fatigue. Then the Unconscious runs amok and tramples all the barriers of respectability that the conscious self has erected. The conscious self has never fully realized that it's up against someone who has known it since childhood. It tends to underrate the invader. Thus, it can be taken by surprise and quickly overrun.

Is it then too late? Thanks to Sigmund Freud—who left Vienna, the city of his dreams, when the Nazis came in 1938 and who died a year later in London—the answer today is no.

No breakdown is permanent if the patient faces up to his dreams, examines them searchingly, seeks professional help where needed, and prepares to confront the childhood friend who has become his Unconscious enemy. For man cannot live by dreams alone, but dreams can help him live with himself.

CHAPTER FOUR:

Dreams That Changed History

Long before Freud, men were governed by dreams. Organized religion, after all, is based partly on what theologians call *visions*. History, too, is rife with examples of the power of positive dreaming.

Many, many years before the birth of Christ, King Astyages of the Medes—ruler of Asia—dreamed that a vine grew from the womb of his daughter and overshadowed all of Asia. By a coincidence, Astyages' daughter had married a Persian and was now exceedingly pregnant.

The king summoned his official dream interpreter, who told him: "Your dream means one thing, oh King of the Medes! Your daughter's child—yea verily, your own grandchild!—will displace you as ruler of all Asia."

Astyages was not about to let this happen, so he sent for a trusted aid, Harpagus. "I beseech you, oh noble and faithful Harpagus," the King began, "to take the child born of my daughter unto your home and slay it there. Thence bury the newborn infant as you please."

The child was born. Scarcely before the proud parents could say in Persian, "It's a boy!", Harpagus snatched the infant from his cradle. He took the baby—named Cyrus—to his home.

"Such a handsome baby!" his wife remarked wistfully. "Can't we keep him, Harpagus my love?"

"No, darling," the noble Harpagus replied. "I cannot betray my King. But, you know what? I can scarcely bring myself to kill an innocent child."

"Listen, Harpagus," his wife said. "You must be careful. First off, this infant is a distant relative of ours

44

by various marriages. Secondly, Astyages is getting old, he has no son, and he probably won't—unless he has a few surprises in him. Agreed?"

"Agreed," said Harpagus.

"Anyway," his wife continued, "when Astyages dies, his crown goes to his daughter. And I know that girl! If she so much as guesses that you killed her son, you are as good as dead, Harpagus. She is a very vindictive person, just like her father."

"But we cannot take the infant into our own family," Harpagus protested. "He would be discovered. Anyway, we have a three-year-old boy of our own. No, Cyrus *must* be killed—but not at my hands!"

"I know a herdsman," said his wife, "who can dispose of anything."

The herdsman relieved Harpagus of his royal burden, but a funny thing happened to him on the way to the slaughter. He took a detour by way of his home to look in on his wife, who was expecting a baby herself. He found his wife a trifle distressed. Her baby had just been stillborn.

"It was a boy," she told her husband sadly. "Just what we've always wanted. Well, we'll have to give it another try, very soon. Say, what have you got there?"

"Matter of fact," said her husband, "a baby boy named Cyrus. But I have to get rid of him fast. He's got royal blood or something."

"He looks mighty healthy to me," the wife remarked, "I'll tell you what: Let's keep this live one and bury the dead one. It makes good sense and nobody'll ever know the difference."

Ten years later, the inevitable happened. Young Cyrus gave offense to one of his social betters and was haled before King Astyages himself for a royal rebuke. Despite a bad case of astigmatism, old Astyages was able to detect a family resemblance. He counted the years on trembling fingers. He recalled that his ill-fated grandson had also been named Cyrus. And he summoned the boy's "father," the herdsman, who confessed all.

Astyages let the herdsman off with a royal tongue-lashing, but he was furious at the noble and faithful Harpagus. Astyages was a devious man. He said nothing. Instead, he summoned Harpagus' thirteen-year-old son to his palace.

Harpagus, Jr., was an only child and a very insecure one. He was particularly nervous about the invitation to come to the palace at once without telling anybody. He had good reason to worry: Upon presenting himself, he was slain and hacked into pieces.

Certain portions of the lad were roasted on the royal hearth; others were boiled in the royal kitchen. That night, Harpagus came to dinner at the palace—as he often did—and was served the flesh of his own son. After they had dined heartily, the host asked Harpagus how he had enjoyed the feast.

"Excessively," Harpagus replied. "You must give my wife the recipe."

With that, King Astyages brought Harpagus a basket containing the head, hands, and feet of his only son. Astyages decided not to take any further action against him: "I am a kindly man, Harpagus. You have been punished enough."

Astyages then summoned his grandson and said:

"Oh, Cyrus, my grandchild, a decade ago I was led to do you a great wrong by a dream that thus far has come to naught. My official dream interpreter, whom I will have beheaded, tells me that it may still come true. But I am too sensitive a person to go through this kind of intrigue again at my age. Instead, I will make things up to you. I will acknowledge my grandfatherhood. I will ship you back to Persia. There you will be re-united with your father and mother. They do not yet know you are alive. Certainly, with them you will live better than you did with that herdsman and his slatternly wife. Begone, oh happy Cyrus!"

Cyrus, however, was not so happy as it appeared to his grandfather. He grew up nursing a grudge against the old man. For good reasons, there was a great deal of family bitterness all around. Not long after Cyrus attained manhood, he led a Persian Revolution that over-threw Astyages. Cyrus took over the throne himself, do-ing such a spectacular job that he soon became known as Cyrus the Great. Cyrus gave Harpagus a good job with his Government. But he did not clap the deposed Astyages into jail, where he belonged. Instead, he kept the senile ex-monarch around the court as a rueful hanger-on and a reminder that, if you are going to heed your dreams, you can't heed them halfway.

Astyages' dream, which certainly altered history, is told by Herodotus in *The Persian Wars*. Cyrus the Great, like his grandfather, was a heavy dreamer. *Once, Cyrus dreamed of making two attempts to catch the sun, which eluded his grasp each time.* His staff dream in-terpreters—known as *magi*—said that each attempt sym-bolized a decade of power. "Thus," they said, "you will reign for twenty years, more or less." Cyrus ruled the Persian Empire from 550 B.C. to 529 B.C.

The man who broke the back of the Persian Empire two centuries later was also heralded by a famous dream.

King Philip of Macedon had married Olympia and made her his Queen. *One night, he had a disturbing dream, in which he saw himself close off his Queen's womb with an official seal, the imprint of which ap-peared to contain a lion.* King Philip went to several dream interpreters, who whispered the usual warnings to watch his wife's conduct carefully. But then he en-countered a highly-paid oracle named Aristandros, who said: "Oh, King of all kings to date! Your dream denotes that your Queen is pregnant, for a seal is never put upon anything that is empty. Rejoice, greatest of kings! The imprint signifies that your son will be a boy of bold and lionlike courage. Mark my words!"

The Queen *was* pregnant, it turned out. When the child came, it *was* a boy. He was Alexander the Great.

When Alexander the Great grew up, he conquered the Persians and burned their capital at Persepolis. But, since he considered himself too busy to dream, his armies carried staff oracles to do the officers' dreaming.

The Chief of the Corps of Oracles was, of course, Aristandros—who had reaped many rewards for predicting Alexander's birth.

One night, despite all his precautions, Alexander the Great had a dream of his own. It came during a crucial period when Alexander was besieging the city of Tyre in vain. He had been considering withdrawing his army. *In his dream, he saw a lecherous man with a horse's ears and tail. The man was cavorting triumphantly.*

The next day, Alexander called in Aristandros and told him his dream. Aristandros had grown fat and cautious, so he began his analysis solemnly:

"All hail, Alexander the Great, greatest of the great! Your dream is easily understandable to the professionally trained and licensed observer. You have seen a satyr. Good day, great ruler!"

"Don't go just yet, Aristandros," said Alexander the Great.

The oracle halted in mid-exit. "Your word, greatest of all rulers, is my command."

"Then tell me: What is a satyr?"

"A satyr, great Alexander the Great, is what you have seen in your dream. It does not exist except in Greek mythology."

"Then what does my dream mean?"

Aristandros thought fast. "Let us look at the word *satyr* itself. In Greek, which is what we speak here, it is *satyros*. Let us now break down the word into its component parts, if we may. *Sa* means *your*. *Tyros* means *Tyre*. Thus: *Your Tyre.*"

"Hmmm," Alexander the Great mused aloud. "In other words, Tyre is mine. Then I must attack!"

"I am licensed only to interpret dreams, not to plot strategy, your Greatness," Aristandros protested. "Therefore, if I may be excused, it is time for my weekly session with the enlisted men's dreams."

But his excuses went unheeded, for Alexander had already renewed the attack on Tyre, which fell before his onslaught. Aristandros the Oracle later claimed much of the credit.

It was ever thus in days of yore. Hecuba anticipated the Trojan War in a disturbing dream. Cicero learned in a dream that he was destined for greatness. If Julius Caesar had heeded the dreams of others, he would not have been in town for the Ides of March. And Hannibal was assured by a dream that he would cross the Alps in the Second Punic War.

A Greek, Babylonian, or Palestinian mother could have had few greater aspirations than for her son to grow up to be an oracle. The job paid well and most dreams were easy to interpret. Some Greek oracles, however, had to make sacrifices: remote towns, lonely caverns, cliffs, gorges, and other places were preferred locations because they were allegedly conducive to dreaming.

When a pilgrim would seek out one of the better dream interpreters, the oracle would listen briefly and then ask several searching questions:

"Was your dream seen or heard?"

"Did it openly foretell the future or was it shrouded in symbolism?"

"Was your dream addressed to you, your relatives, your friends, your enemies, your country, or the world at large?"

"What circumstances in your life related to those in the dream?"

"Do you love your parents? Your children? Your spouse? Others?"

"What is your occupation? Income? Cost of home?"

"What are your five principal worries?"

If the oracle could not then interpret the dream or if the dreamer was wealthy, he would be invited into the oracle's temple. There, after paying a fee, he would be allowed to fast for a whole day. "This means purification," the oracle would explain. Then a ram would be sacrificed to a local god at the patient's expense. Afterwards, the patient would go to sleep in the temple. If he had any dreams, he would relate them to the oracle, who would interpret them.

If he did not dream or if the oracle could not interpret his dreams, the patient would be invited to stay on for another night—at an additional charge. Greek oracles soon discovered that wealthy people had the fewest and most difficult dreams.

At Epidaurus, the priests of the temple not only interpreted dreams, but they also prescribed for the dreamer's afflictions. Sometimes, the priests actually performed cures. In his classic volume, *A History of Dreams,* A. J. J. Ratcliff has observed rather cynically:

> The machinery of dream oracles is obvious. Potent gases, or oth᷍ ᷍ributory influences stimulated vivid dreams. The frightful aspect of wild and secluded places inspired awe. Preoccupation with religious ideas lent a divine color to the experience. Fasting and narcotic potions increased the ecstasy. And then faith, strengthened by the prestige of the oracle and the manipulations of the diseased place by the priests, brought about the cures.

In Palestine and Babylon, dream interpreters had the prestige of doctors. They were consulted far more frequently. After interpreting a dream, an oracle would also prescribe a special fast. By the third century A.D., there were twenty-four authorized dream interpreters in the city limits of Jerusalem.

The prophet Mohammed, beloved to Moslems everywhere, once dreamed that he visited Heaven, took a guided tour, conferred at length with important angels, and then returned to his body. Upon awakening, Mohammed found that he had been asleep for less than a minute.

Mohammed had his detractors. One of them was the Egyptian Sultan of Skept, known to his harem as "The Doubting Sultan." When the Sultan of Skept was told of Mohammed's dream, he remarked, "Now I've heard everything!! Mohammed's gone too far this time! Mountains will not come to him, so why should he be able to go to Heaven and back in less than a minute? It can't be done! Bah!"

Upon hearing the Doubting Sultan's grunt, his religious tutor, Abou ben Chaimen, came running. "You must not say things like that," he cautioned his employer. Abou ben Chaimen offered to prove that anything is possible in a dream. He had a large basin of water brought to the Sultan's chamber.

"I've already bathed today, thank you," the Sultan told Abou. "And for your insolence in suggesting I need a bath, I ought to have you emasculated."

But Abou asked him to plunge his head into the basin and then withdraw it as quickly as possible. The Sultan of Skept did so.

As soon as he was underwater, he found himself on a lonely shore that was not his own. He was hungry. Even a Sultan, however, is just another foreigner when he ventures abroad. He had to find work. Wandering in the woods, he met some lumbermen. They offered him a job. He worked at it for several years, married his foreman's daughter, and sired fourteen children. But, when his wife died, his father-in-law the foreman demoted him to assistant lumberjack. The man from Skept quit in protest. Unfortunately, he was unable to find equivalent work in the lumber industry. He took odd jobs, but he was never able to regain his feet financially. One day, strolling by the sea, he decided to drown himself.

At this point, the Sultan lifted his head from the basin. His tutor, Abou ben Chaimen, handed him a towel and said: "You were in there less than a minute. All that transpired occurred during one deep breath."

The Sultan of Skept spat out some water and then announced: "I believe!"

From then on, he was active in Moslem causes. Mohammed never had to fear his opposition. And, since the Doubting Sultan was a powerful figure of his time, it was fortunate for Moslems that Abou ben Chaimen won him over through a dream—plus, I suspect, a little bit of hypnotic suggestion.

Eventually, the Sultan of Skept became known all

over Egypt as the Dreaming Sultan. He also became a
much more potent lover, according to his harem records.

In seventh-century England, a group of tavern row-
dies hoisted high their flagons and—to mark each round
—one of the merrymakers would invent a toast or
a verse. At this tavern in the town there was a bashful
youth named Caedmon. He had been born in a stable.
He now worked in a stable. Rather than have his im-
provised verse hooted down, he retreated to his stable.
Caedmon fell asleep in the hay. *He dreamed that "a
person" appeared and commanded: "Caedmon, sing me
something."* Caedmon obeyed, went back to the tavern,
delivered his song, and went on to become *the* Muse of
English Verse. Caedmon has the very first entries in
Bartletts *Familiar Quotations* (1951 edition) plus a
footnote that this was the beginning of English poetry.

Scandinavians have always dreamed like mad! In
Caedmon's time, a Norwegian badman named Hrolf
planned to invade England. But then he dreamed of
defeat. Instead, he attacked Paris. He had more success
there—for a while. Eventually, however, he was de-
ported.

Another Norwegian, Ingismund, decided to colonize
Iceland. He had better luck than Hrolf because he was
very cautious.

To assure his journey's success, Ingismund had three
Finnish prisoners placed in a hut. He visited them there
and told them: "When you sleep, I want your souls to
set out for Iceland. I want you to find a district where
Norwegians can live as they live at home. And, when
your souls get back, I want the exact locations—
or else."

"But, sir," one of the prisoners inquired through an
interpreter, "with all due respect, how do we know our
souls will find the way?"

"That," said the noble Viking, "is your problem."

The three prisoners went into seclusion, conferred
briefly, fell asleep, awoke seventy-one hours later, con-

ferred briefly, and sent for Ingismund. Miraculously, it seemed, their three dreams were identical.

Following their instructions, Ingismund set out to colonize Iceland. There were many discrepancies between dreams and reality, but, by adhering to all advice that proved applicable and making snap decisions of his own, Ingismund arrived safely.

When Dante died in 1321, his records were a mess. Like many poets, he had been meaning to do something about his files. Like poets and peasants alike, he had never found the time. To his son Jacopo fell the task of putting his father's papers in order.

One night, Dante visited his son's dreams and asked —rather skeptically—if his son had anything on his mind. Jacopo replied that he had been looking high and low for thirteen missing cantos of Dante's Divine Comedy. Dante directed Jacopo to a place where his son had looked twice before.

When he awoke, Jacopo checked. This time, the papers were there.

If Dante had told this story, it would have been hailed as another masterpiece. But, when Jacopo told it, his fellow Italians waved their arms angrily.

"You never looked there before," one critic assured him.

"You found it long ago and hid it, hoping to command a better price after it had been 'lost' for a few years," said a shrewd old merchant of Venice.

The young man's cousin Vitello was even more blunt: "You are a liar, Jacopo! You've always been a liar because your father didn't bring you up right."

The only person who believed him was a gullible Neapolitan street singer named Renata. "You dreamed it, Jacopo, but *why* did you dream it?" she said intensely. "I'll tell you why: because you'd done a careless job of searching and something deep down inside you—something bigger than both of us—told you that this was the place where you should have looked. It's all terribly clear to me."

Jacopo put his hands to his ears and kept them there for days. He also wept copiously. It is often this way with the sons of famous fathers. Nobody gives them much credit for anything—even dreaming.

Joan of Arc had it easier than Jacopo Dante because she started out as a fifteenth-century nobody from Domremy, a town that France had forgotten. Unhampered by family and encouraged by saintly voices that only she could hear, Joan became a leader of men and a kingmaker *par excellence*. But then a ghastly mistake was made. Joan of Arc was burned to death for various offenses, including having dared to dream heretically.

You cannot punish a girl for dreaming—particularly when she is religiously inclined. Twenty-five years after her death, Joan was vindicated. Today, she is a full-fledged saint.

Benvenuto Cellini, a sixteenth-century Italian rake, never was a candidate for sainthood, but he achieved immortality through his sculpture and writing.

One night, he was languishing in an Italian prison when he dreamed that a handsome youth came to him and said: "Cellini, knowest thou who lent thee that body which thou wouldst have spoiled before its time?"

Cellini answered hesitantly that he thought the answer might be God.

"That is right," said the youth. "So then thou hast contempt for His handiwork through this thy will to spoil it? Commit thyself unto His guidance, Cellini, and lose not hope in His great goodness."

Cellini had been thinking seriously about killing himself. Instead, he decided to live on. To while away the time, he took up serious writing.

Every night thereafter, he reported, "I was visited with the gladdest and most pleasant dreams that could possibly be imagined."

His dreams made his prison stay bearable. When he craved sunlight in his darkened dungeon, he dreamed of sunlight. For Cellini, imprisonment almost became *la dolce vita*.

When he was freed, he resumed his notorious ways. If, however, a dream had not stopped Cellini from destroying himself, history might have been deprived of some great art and a racy autobiography.

British history has a certain dreamlike quality all its own. The Duke of Buckingham anticipated the beheading of King Charles I in a dream. But, at the time, beheadings were not uncommon in dream life *or* waking life.

Richard the Lion-Hearted was off crusading in the Holy Land when he dreamed that his kingdom was being divided behind his back. Upon his return, he found that his dream was all too true.

Oliver Cromwell was saved from a murderer by a timely dream. And Henry IV envisioned in Part I of an epic dream that he would be assassinated.

Sir Thomas White, Lord Mayor of London, was dozing in the shade of three tree trunks when a dream ordered him to build a college. A venerable British superstition insists that dreams dreamed in the shade of three tree trunks must be heeded. Sir Thomas had no choice but to endow a college, which turned out to be St. John's College of Oxford University.

Musical history owes much to dreams. Richard Wagner, who composed some of the world's most breast-beating music, found himself stymied by the prelude for his immortal *Das Rheingold*. There was no suitable theme to be found! Wagner toiled unavailingly for hours, then fell asleep exhausted. *He dreamed of a flood. The turbulent waters suggested a series of chords.* These chords later found their way into Wagner's "Prelude in E-flat Major" to *Das Rheingold*. Wagner later wrote: "The stream of life was not to flow to me from without, but from within."

Giuseppi Tartini was a temperamental eighteenth-century violinist who decided he was ready to compose his masterpiece. Unfortunately, he could find none within him.

"I would sell my soul to the Devil for the idea for one really good masterpiece," Tartini told himself one day.

The Devil has spies everywhere. *That night, Tartini dreamed that he did sell his soul to the Devil. In the dream, he also handed his violin to the Devil, who said, "I would like you to tell me, Signor Tartini, if I'm as good a fiddler as my servant Nero says I am."*

The Devil was indeed a talented chap, as Tartini later wrote in his memoirs:

> How great was my astonishment when I heard him play with consummate skill a sonata of such exquisite beauty as surpassed the boldest flights of my imagination! I felt enraptured, transported, enchanted. My breath was taken away and I awoke.

Tartini rushed to his violin and tried to repeat the sounds of music. He was only partially successful. The piece he composed—which, to give the Devil his due, became known as "The Devil's Sonata"—was hailed as Tartini's masterpiece. But people who make deals with the Devil (even in their dreams) are seldom satisfied. Tartini wrote: "How far below the one I had heard in my dream!"

In an incident similar to Tartini's—although influenced by opium rather than the Devil—the poet Samuel Taylor Coleridge dreamed an entire 300-line poem. When he arose, he managed to jot down the first forty-five lines from memory, but then a traveling salesman knocked on the door and interrupted Coleridge's work. When he returned to his desk, he was able to remember only eight or ten more lines. Even so, this was the birth of Coleridge's opulent poem, *Kubla Khan*, which begins

> In Xanadu did Kubla Khan
> A stately pleasure-dome decree.

Another author who, like Coleridge, became involved with drugs and dreams (but not, thank Heaven, with traveling salesmen) was Charlotte Brontë. She wrote *Jane Eyre*, a novel that later gained fame as an Orson Welles movie. Charlotte Brontë had a probelm that afflicts most fiction writers: *How do you describe a place or event that you have never seen?* Her solution was to ponder such a problem just before going to bed. At night, she would dream of it. In the morning, she would write it.

In her novel *Villette*, Miss Brontë described opium addiction so effectively that she received fan mail from drug addicts everywhere. They were convinced that the genteel lady herself was hooked! Charlotte Brontë, however, insisted that she had never once tried opium. Her sisters, her friends, and even her worst enemies confirmed this. Charlotte Brontë made literary history on her own merit, but her sales were certainly not hindered by her loyal following of dope fiends.

Still another literary dreamer was the late William Makepeace Thackeray. He had just written a sensational novel about a girl named Becky Sharp. His publishers thought it would sell if it had a catchy title.

"I say, it wouldn't be amiss to call this little opus *Becky Sharp*, would it now?" one of the junior editors piped up.

"Ahem!" said a senior editor, whose wisdom everybody was quick to see. "A title like *Becky Sharp* would make people think Bill had written just another women's novel—like *Jane Eyre*."

The consensus of the meeting eventually was that a title like *Rapacious Becky* would sell the book—for all the wrong reasons, perhaps. But people would buy it!

In the nick of time, Thackeray had a dream. When it was over, he reported: "I jumped out of bed in the middle of the night and ran three times around my room, uttering as I went, '*Vanity Fair! Vanity Fair! Vanity Fair!*' "

In the morning, his publisher said dubiously: "*Vanity*

Fair? I wonder if that might not sound a bit too like one of those vanity press novels that are published at the author's own expense."

But Thackeray was adamant—as only a man named Makepeace can be! His title stuck. *Vanity Fair* went on to become a best-seller.

Even outside literature, the nineteenth century was dominated by dreams. Take, for example, five notable facets of the 1800's:

Invention: Elias Howe was hung up on a seemingly unmendable snag. It began to look as if he would never finish inventing the sewing machine. He just could not get the needle action to work properly. After a hard day's work, Howe fell asleep with a throbbing headache. Appropriately, he dreamed of jungle drums. Then he saw natives carrying long lances. The lances had holes in their spearheads. Fortunately, Freud had not yet been invented, so Howe was able to ponder his dream's meaning on a pragmatic level. He realized that his dream was telling him that the best way for a machine to thread a needle was through a hole in the needle's point. Howe thus solved his needle action problem, although his headache persisted.

Fossilology: Professor Louis Agassiz, a naturalist, was worrying about the shape of a fish fossil that had been vaguely outlined in a marble slab he was working on. For three nights in a row, however, Professor Agassiz dreamed of the full fish. On the basis of his dream, he located the complete fossil.

Science: For centuries, Science had been seeking a pat formula that would explain the arrangement of atoms within a molecule of benzene. A German chemist, Dr. Friedrich August Kekule von Stradonitz, was determined to make a name for himself. One night, he dreamed of atoms tumbling chaotically before his eyes. Suddenly, the atoms combined to form a snake, which then proceeded to bite its own tail. Like most German scientists, Dr. Kekule (as he was called) seldom dreamed of snakes. Sensing that he was on to something big, he soon realized that he had dreamed of the shape of the Benzene Ring. Science took a giant step on its march to total destruction and the name of Dr. Friedrich August Kekule von Stradonitz was enshrined for as long as man will prevail.

Science Fiction (which some critics consider outside the pale of literature): Robert Louis Stevenson had been belaboring an idea about two beings that dwell in one man's body. His labors had come to naught but a rejection slip—too unbelievable, an editor told him. Soon after the initial shock of refusal had worn off, Stevenson dreamed of a suitable story line. His new plot was accepted and his story was called *Dr. Jekyll and Mr. Hyde*. . . . Stevenson himself was living proof that at least two beings exist within each of us. He constantly referred to his "Brownies, God bless them!, who do one-half my work for me while I am still fast asleep." Stevenson also urged his critics to blame his weaker efforts on his Brownies and to praise their collaborator when a story succeeded.

Assyriology: The nineteenth century was perhaps the Golden Era of Assyriology, which is the study of antiquities and language of ancient Assyria. Most good colleges prided themselves on their Assyriology departments. In 1893, the University of Pennsylvania's crack Assyriologist was Dr. H. V. Hilprecht. As anyone who has read a fascinating article in the March, 1896, issue of *Psychological Review* will tell you, Dr. Hilprecht had been trying in vain to decipher two stray fragments of tablet. One Saturday night, he fell asleep and dreamed that a long and lanky priest ambled over to him with the news that both fragments should be joined almost like pieces of a jigsaw puzzle. Hilprecht awoke. To make sure that he would never forget what he had just dreamed, he awakened his wife and told her to remember it. (This is known as the Scientific Method.) The next morning, he went to work and found that the lean and hungry-looking priest had been dead right. Hilprecht went on to great heights in the field of Assyriology. It is to be hoped that his wife went back to sleep.

As for contemporary dreams, history has yet to write its final chapter on the Twentieth Century. But here are already a few early entries destined to stand unchallenged:

. . . Victor Herbert composed his unforgettable song, "Kiss Me Again," in a dream.

. . . William Archer, a playwright, found the plot for *The Green Goddess* in a dream. There have been better plays and better playwrights, but among theatre people Archer is remembered for such virtuoso displays of ingenuity.

. . . Juan Vincente Gomez, who once made Venezuela safe for dictators named Gomez, scored an early victory thanks to a dream. Dreaming that his arch-enemy Hernandez would pause at a chapel near a crossroads, Gomez went there and ambushed the unlucky but devout Hernandez.

. . . An electrically controlled anti-aircraft gun—which was later adopted for use by the United States Army in its eternal battle against totalitarianism—was conceived in its inventor's dreams.

. . . Dr. Otto Loewi, a Nobel Prize-winning scientist, credited a dream with recalling a hunch that had crossed his mind seventeen years earlier. Applying that insight anew, he rushed into his laboratory and dissected a frog. This experiment—on the transmission of the nervous impulse—became known as Dr. Loewi's most notable scientific achievement.

With the emergence of a new African nation nearly every day, it is not hard to predict that dreams will have growing impact on world history. As provincial witch doctors evolve into statesmen, dreams may some day affect the balance of power in the United Nations. What results may not be a Utopia, but perhaps a world dominated by dreams will be a world in which all men can re-create themselves equal . . . where no passport will be required . . . where there will be a total lack of discrimination . . . and where free association will be encouraged. Perhaps not.

CHAPTER FIVE:

Prophetic Dreams

My good friend Professor Josiah Carberry was in New York for a day and I invited him to my home. As usual, Carberry came to scoff but allowed that he would remain to eat.

"And what particular aspect of dreams are you tampering with now?" he inquired with customary directness.

"I'm trying to shed light on prophetic dreams," I replied.

"Prophetic dreams? Do you mean dreams by Elijah and that crowd?"

"Only in part. Not exclusively. I include all sorts of prophetic dreams. Lincoln's, for example."

"Abraham Lincoln the President?" Carberry asked.

"The same," I said. "A few days before he was assassinated, Lincoln dreamed that he was wandering through the White House when he came upon a sentry standing guard over a coffin in the East Room. Lincoln asked the soldier who was dead. The soldier told him, 'The President. He was killed by an assassin.' After that, there was a wail of grief from the mourners."

Carberry lit his pipe slowly—as he often does when he has something important to say.

After a long moment, he spoke: "You know, my good man, with all due respect for Mr. Lincoln, that's a lot of eyewash!"

"I beg your pardon," I said in the slightly strained tone of one who has been baited before by Carberry.

Carberry thumped his pipe against my coffee table,

missed the ash tray with his ashes, and continued calmly: "You see, Lincoln knew damned well that his life was in utmost danger. All he had to do was scan his mail! Any President knows that he is hated by a good many of his countrymen. Lincoln, in particular, was hated because he had licked the South. Remember, the country was crawling with Civil War buffs at the time."

"I hadn't thought of that," I observed.

"If Lincoln's dream had any meaning at all, he was trying to convince himself that people really would miss him after his death. Hence the wail of grief. His dream was very understandable and properly Freudian, but no more prophetic than any other dream of death."

I was a trifle peeved at my guest's skepticism, so I tried to squelch his ridicule of prophetic dreams once and for all.

"Carberry, if a dream by Abraham Lincoln won't impress you, how would you feel about a dream by J. Cannon Middleton?"

"Who?"

"Mr. Middleton booked passage on the *Titanic* for its maiden voyage. A few nights later, he dreamed that the ship was sinking and its passengers were swimming for dear life."

"My, my," Carberry purred.

"Mr. Middleton laughed off the dream, but he had it again the next night. Finally, he cancelled his reservation. The ship was considered unsinkable, but four nights after it had sailed without Mr. Middleton aboard . . ."

"I've seen enough movies. I know the rest of the story," Carberry interrupted. "But have you ever thought that fifteen hundred people who were aboard that ship might have had dreams that said, 'Take the *Titanic*'?"

"Well, we'll never know about *their* dreams."

"Precisely! But, after any big disaster, all sorts of people remember dreams that suddenly assume meaning. We dream about life, so anything that happens in a dream bears some relation to waking life. But that's about all you can say for Mr. Middleton's dream." He pointed his pipe at me and said: "You remember, of course, what Voltaire said about prophetic dreams."

"No, I don't. I imagine he was pretty sardonic about them."

"Truth is often sardonic. Anyway, Voltaire said: 'Dreams that have come to pass are always predictions which no one can doubt, no account being taken of dreams which are never fulfilled. One dream accomplished has more effect than a hundred that fail.' "

"All right, Carberry," I retorted, "since you've gone back to the bookshelf for a little ammunition, I'll do the same." I pulled down a slender volume containing the collected works of the ancient Greek poet Aceius, who wrote:

> Dreams are in general reflex images
> Of things that men in waking hours have known;
> But sometimes dreams of loftier character
> Rise in the tranced soul, inspired by Jove,
> Prophetic of the future.

After I had read it aloud, there was a hush.

"Well, Carberry?"

"I will answer your question with a question of my own: Do you call *that* poetry?"

"What about its meaning?"

"Every bit as obscure as the poet himself. Now, as the beloved Plutarch observes so pungently . . ."

Rather than swap quotes, I decided to confront Carberry immediately with a classic case history that had baffled psychiatry for many years:

"A man lived in a house that had white grapes growing on a vine outside. One night, he dreamed that the vine was filled with black grapes instead of white ones. A month later, his wife—who'd been pregnant—gave birth to a Negro child."

"And both husband and wife were white people, I presume?" Carberry said.

"Beyond a doubt. This happened in Mississippi, where people are very precise about such matters."

"Well, then," said Carberry, "that is the easiest one

you've flung at me yet. The husband was suspicious that his wife had been unfaithful. He had even suspected that she was bestowing her favors upon a Negro. Being a diehard white supremacist, his conscious mind rejected the idea—but even a Southerner has a subconscious that cannot be repressed entirely. In his dream, he was contemplating—symbolically, that is—what he wouldn't admit to himself in broad daylight."

"Carberry, you act so knowledgeable that one would almost suspect you were there."

"I am a man of the world—thanks to traveling fellowships. In fact, the vast number of grants that I have acquired seem to have earned me a small reputation as an academic vagabond. But thus far I haven't had a Fulbright Scholarship to Mississippi. The White Citizens Council, I'm told, gives liberal grants—but only to northbound Negro scholars."

"If I remember your picture postals correctly, your most recent traveling fellowship was to Egypt. Did you get to visit the Sphinx?"

"Ah, yes."

"And did you happen to notice that between her paws there was an inscription on a slab of granite?"

"Yes, yes," Carberry replied. "Something about a dream by Thutmose IV."

"Thutmose? Is that the one the Egyptologists call 'King Tut?' " my wife inquired brightly, as she entered with a pitcher of martinis.

"No," Carberry replied. "That was Tutankhamen. Thutmose IV was a couple of centuries ahead of him."

"Anyway," I continued, "back in the sixteenth century B.C., when Thutmose was a young princeling, he went hunting and took a nap in the shadow of the Sphinx."

"Very restful place," Carberry remarked nostalgically.

"It must have been, for Thutmose dreamed that the Sphinx sphoke—excuse me!—spoke to him. She said that if he cleared away the sand that, over the years, had been burying her paws, she would reward him with the crown of Egypt."

"And?"

"Thutmose awoke, obeyed her instructions, and later became the King of Upper and Lower Egypt. Now how's that for a prophetic dream?"

My wife cleared her throat and said: "It seems to me that, even if he'd never had that dream, Prince Titmouse or whatever his name was would have succeeded to the throne."

Carberry chimed in: "And if he had the dream but did not heed it, he was still destined to grow up to be King Thutmose IV. His destiny was foolproof."

"That may be," I said, "but the fact that a dream's prophecy is an easy one does nothing to refute it as a prophetic dream." Still, I appeared to have suffered a setback, so I changed the subject gracefully: "Speaking of royalty, William the Conqueror's son—whose name was William Rufus—used to like to go hunting, just like Thutmose."

"Indeed," said Carberry.

"One night, William Rufus dreamed that he was injured. Less than a month later, he went on a hunting trip and was killed by a stray arrow."

Carberry was unimpressed: "Any man who likes to hunt should be required to have prophetic dreams. In fact, you and the National Safety Council ought to get together and make all hunters stay home and dream. Then maybe we could put an end to all those legalized murders in the woods. Hunting accidents, bah! Do you know what the great American epitaph is? It's *'I thought he was a moose.'* "

"Professor Carberry," my wife said gently, "I think you're trying to divert attention from the prophetic dream my husband was telling us. I would like to hear your explanation."

Carberry drew himself up starchily and declared with a professorial air of finality: "I have said all I am going to say about hunting or dreams of hunting."

"Since you're our guest," I said sarcastically, "we'll have to abide by your rules. But allow me to tell you another story—a non-hunting story—about British royalty."

Carberry refilled his martini glass and proposed a toast: "To British royalty! Now let's hear your story."

I began, "You've heard of Lady Jane Grey, I trust."

"Yes," said Carberry with a grisly chuckle. "England's Queen for a Day."

"Nine days," I said. "Back in the sixteenth century. And I don't think your remark was the least bit funny."

"I thought it was," said my wife. "Good taste, no! Funny, yes!"

I told the story: "The night before she was beheaded, Lady Jane dreamed that all the beautiful treetops on her family estate had been chopped off. And, sure enough . . ."

"Don't tell me," Carberry interrupted. "Let me guess! The very next day, she was beheaded."

"There's much more to it than that. A day after Lady Jane was beheaded, the Grey family's woodsman chopped off all the treetops on the estate. What do you say to that, Carberry?"

"A fine gesture of loyalty," he said infuriatingly. "With the exception of Lady Chatterley and her gamekeeper, you seldom find that sort of passionate employer-employee relationship nowadays."

"I might add that the woodsman could not have known about Lady Jane's dream when he took his action. It was several days before the news of Lady Jane's dream could have reached him."

Carberry coughed and then said: "Have you ever thought, old man, that chopping off the treetops might have been a traditional gesture of mourning in the Grey family? The woodsman knew it. Lady Jane knew it. Everybody seemed to know it except mythmakers like you."

"Looking at the story impartially," my wife observed, "I see it my husband's way."

"Then I consider myself outnumbered, if not outwitted," Carberry said with a slight bow.

While my wife mixed a fresh batch of martinis, I told

Carberry about a recent symposium conducted by the London *Evening Star*. Readers were asked to submit experiences relating to what the newspaper called "second sight."

"I call it hindsight," said Carberry. "That's what prophetic dreams are."

I ignored his thrust and handed him a clipping from the *Star:*

> I was working in a hosiery factory in Leicester overlooking a main road. One day when I awoke, I knew I had had a particularly troubled dream, but could not recall much about it. During the afternoon my dream suddenly became clear to me. In it I had seen a bus crash into the workroom in which I was employed. I called to me those of my workmates who were nearest to the outer wall and told them of my dream. I had hardly finished when my dream came true. A bus crashed into the wall, but none of my workmates was injured.

"There's always one prophetic dreamer in every factory," Carberry declared. "You usually find him in charge of coffee breaks or organizing unions. If he can't say 'I told you so'—and one can't very well blame one's employers for sticking their factory in the way of a bus —he can at least say, 'I dreamed this very thing last night.' Bah!" With that, Carberry tore my clipping in half.

I dared not risk another clipping in Carberry's hands, so I read the next one to him. It concerned a man who was temporarily unable to pay a small amount to a very persistent creditor. At his wit's end, he dropped into troubled sleep the night before his creditor's final deadline. He dreamed that his milkman delivered money instead of milk. The next morning, he called his dairy to check over his accounts. He found that he had been overcharged and had overpaid a sum large enough to cover his debt. The money was refunded cheerfully and promptly, thus enabling the dreamer to thwart disaster.

"Christopher Morley said it better," Carberry declared. "He said: 'Truth, like milk, arrives in the dark.'" And Carberry could not be drawn into any further discussion of the incident.

My wife filled the conversational gap by telling us a story about a dream that a friend of hers had a few days before getting married:

The woman dreamed that she boarded a bus and gave the driver a transfer. "What time is it, lady?" the driver asked her. She replied that it was two minutes before five. The driver, who looked like her fiancé, then remarked, "You're lucky, lady. This transfer you gave me expires at five." The lady said nothing, but walked to the back of the bus, which had no empty seats. A dapper-looking man, who also resembled her fiancé, looked up from his seat, tipped his hat politely, and said, "Won't you sit down?" But he made no offer to give her his seat. While she was wondering if the man wanted her to sit on his lap, the driver summoned her to the front of the bus. "It's one minute after five now, lady. Your transfer's no good any more," the driver told her. She paid the full fare and returned to the back of the bus, where the dapper man kept suggesting that she sit down. At regular intervals, the driver would make her pay the full fare. Eventually, she wearied of shuttling between the front and the back of the bus, so she got off at an intersection with which she was unfamiliar. A white-gloved policeman, who looked like her fiancé, was directing traffic there. She asked him for directions, but he said nothing. Instead, as she spoke, he reached out and plucked the skin of her neck the way a musician plucks a guitar. After he had done this several times, she lost her voice. She ran away and sought sanctuary in a theatre that was featuring "GRETA GARBO in Rudyard Kipling's The Light That Failed."

At this point, Carberry interrupted: "I've seen every Garbo picture, but I don't remember that one."

"Garbo wasn't in it," my wife told him. Then she concluded her dream narration:

The woman dashed into the theatre without buying a ticket. Pursued by the cashier, the doorman, the manager (who resembled her fiancé) and a platoon of ushers, she ran to the front of the auditorium. Standing before the giant screen—and looking for all the world

*like a tiny speck on the huge image of Garbo's face—
she managed to gasp a frantic plea: "HELP!"*

"A hair-raising story," Carberry commented, "and
one that involves two of my favorite people—Garbo
and Kipling."

My wife added: "Clearly it was a warning to the
dreamer that she should not get married. But she dis-
regarded the dream, went ahead with her plans, and
was divorced in ˙ ˙˙ than a year."

"Because of an argument over a bus transfer? Over
Garbo? Over Kipling?" Carberry inquired.

"I don't know *why*," my wife admitted. "Incom-
patibility, I guess."

"Then the dream is meaningless," Carberry declared.
"Some half-a-million Americans will get divorced this
year without any help or hindrance from dreams."

Seeing my wife go ominously silent, I intervened:
"Speaking of Kipling, as we were a moment ago, are you
still devoted to him, Carberry?"

"Slavishly!" he replied. "I pride myself on being something of an authority on the man. If you can dream and
not make dreams your master, you're a better man than
I am, Gunga Din!"

Thus encouraged (if that was Carberry's intention),
I related the following:

Kipling once dreamed that he was in a stone-floored
ancient hall. A man approached and asked, "May I
have a word with you?"

Not long after his dream, Kipling happened to visit
Westminster Abbey, which has a stone floor. There, he
was accosted by a stranger, who began, "May I have a
word with you?"

Carberry chortled over his martini and then said:

"A man as well traveled and observant as Mr. Rudyard Kipling must have encountered several stone floors
a month. And, when one is a celebrated author, all
sorts of people—parsons, physicians and particularly
illiterates who haven't read your books—are always coming over and asking to have a word with you. I, myself,

as the author of one or two scholarly monographs that have attracted no little attention . . ."

Desperately trying to head off a stultifyingly pedantic Carberry monologue about monographs, I interrupted: "Do you believe in Dickens?"

"Not so much as I believe in Kipling or Santa Claus, but I believe."

"On a Thursday night, Charles Dickens dreamed that he saw a lady in a red shawl. He had never seen her before. She introduced herself, 'I am Miss Napier.' On Friday night, two friends came to visit Dickens. They brought a lady with them. She had a red shawl and her name was Miss Napier."

"What else could it have been?" Carberry asked rhetorically. "On Wednesday or Thursday afternoon, one of Dickens' friends undoubtedly called up and said, 'Charlie, old chap, we'll pop over on Friday night. But don't walk around in your shorts because we may bring old Rosie with us. . . . Rosie? You've met Rosie, haven't you? Rosie Napier . . . That's right, the lady in red. . . . Oh, you've never met her, but you've heard me talking about her? Well, I think you'll like her.' "

"How come Dickens didn't remember this conversation?" I asked.

"Oh, a man like Dickens must have had his mind on bigger things," Carberry replied. "But Dickens, like any other literary man, had a subconscious that was intrigued by the prospect of meeting a lady in red."

"Dickens also had some perspective on dreams," I added, striding to my bookshelf. I took down *David Copperfield* and read Carberry this:

> We have all had some experience of a feeling that comes over us occasionally, of what we are saying and doing having been said or done before, in a remote time, of having been surrounded, dim ages ago, by the same faces, objects, and circumstances, of our knowing perfectly what will be said next, as if we suddenly remembered it.

"I know what he means!" my wife exclaimed. "It happens to me all the time."

"Even you can't deny having had this kind of experience, Carberry," I said.

"Certainly not! What Dickens says is very interesting. It might make me believe in reincarnation. But not in prophetic dreams!"

"Look, Carberry," I persisted. "We dream of things and then they happen. That's the only sane explanation for these recognitions."

"Nonsense! I confess to having been a pallbearer at a funeral. And while I was bearing my heavy burden I thought, 'I have been here before.' "

"And had you?"

"No. It was my first funeral."

"Then you must have been there before in a prophetic dream."

"I think not. Naturally, this feeling of recognition was most disturbing to me. After I had finished up my pallbearing stint, I thought it over. I realized that I had seen too many newsreels of funerals."

"Is that your only explanation?"

"Well, similar things seem to happen to me when I have drunk too much coffee, worked too hard, or had nervous stomach. It has to do with nerves, not prophecy."

"Professor Carberry," my wife declared, "you cannot cure prophetic dreams with Pepto-Bismol."

"Then perhaps I'll try another martini," he said, pouring himself a drink. "And allow me to cite the findings of Mr. Havelock Ellis, the noted sexologist, psychologist, and dream debunker. Ellis said that prophetic dreams need not be discussed in detail. Why? Because they're usually fallacious. If one or two do appear to come true, either the 'prophecy' is based on a failure of memory or the later 'recognition' is caused by one of two factors—the dream's emotional preparation or the dreamer's concentrated expectation. If one element of a prophecy comes true, you tend to surrender to the rest of it. I know of a lady who went to a fortune teller and learned that she would meet a tall, dark gigolo for whom she would forsake her husband and her children, take to drink, and lead a debauched life. Well, two years later, she happened to meet a gigolo. If it hadn't been for the prophecy, she would have ignored him. But having met him, she ran away with him."

Since Carberry had quoted Havelock Ellis, I tried to match him citation for citation: "Ellis also writes about a girl who dreamed that she had swallowed molten lead. When she woke up, she felt all right. A few hours later, however, she came down with a severe case of tonsillitis. Make something out of that, Carberry."

"I shall make a molehill where you would make a mountain," my guest assured me. "This particular dreamer must have realized inwardly that she had tonsillitis. But, as Ellis would be the first to tell you, this dreamer—like most young girls—had a keen mind in a sluggish body."

"You," my wife informed Carberry, "are a woman-hater."

"Nonsense," Carberry replied. "I dislike most people regardless of race, creed, color, or sex."

"Anyone who resists the meaning of dreams must hate himself even more than he hates others," I observed astutely.

"I believe in dream interpretation," Carberry insisted, "but not in miracles or pat solutions."

It would be presumptuous to relate the remainder of our pre-dinner cocktail chatter. Suffice it to say that we served up two more martinis (which Carberry succeeded in downing) and nine more prophetic dreams (which Carberry attempted to destroy forever). The dreams—in summary form, followed by Carberry's analyses—were as follows:

The Dream: In 1906, a San Francisco pharmacist dreamed of catastrophe for two consecutive nights. He warned his friends. On the day after his second dream, a great earthquake destroyed much of San Francisco—including the dreaming druggist.

Carberry: "Your druggist was obviously a worry wart, a perpetual false alarmist, and a chronic dreamer. He undoubtedly dreamed of six disasters a night. But, after a man dies, everyone invariably speaks well of him. His acquaintances remembered a few of his dreams that, by the long arm of coincidence, possessed a semblance of accuracy. Obviously, even the druggist himself did not put much faith in his dreams. If he did, he would have left town before the earthquake struck."

The Dream: A French Duke dreamed of watching a double funeral—his own and a friend's. The friend scoffed, but died soon after of pneumonia. The Duke attended the funeral, where he was assassinated.

Carberry: "The dreamer was a dead Duke from the moment he related his dream. He must have known that his friend's health was weak and vulnerable. And when he mentioned his dream, it must have reminded his enemies that there's no better place to lie in ambush than in a cemetery."

The Dream: A ferris-wheel attendant dreamed that he had been caught in a door and had lost a leg. Alarmed by this vision, he called in sick. That night, he encountered his boss on the boardwalk. The boss rebuked him but told him to get to work and fix the wheel. It had become immobilized when a car door had jammed. The attendant had no choice but to climb up and take a look at the stuck door. While he was aloft, a drunk came along down below and insisted on riding the wheel right then and there. The owner tried to eject him. During the struggle, the drunk lurched against the main control switch. The ferris wheel began going around and around. By the time it had been brought to a halt, the attendant's left leg was so badly mangled that it had to be removed.

Carberry: "The attendant knew he had been performing a sloppy job of maintenance. His dream merely warned him of the danger that he had ignored in his waking hours."

The Dream: When she was ten, a friend of my wife's dreamed that her mother was walking along the Champs-Elysées in Paris. The dreamer tried to follow, but her mother said, "Don't run after me. Daddy needs you." When she woke up, her father told her that her mother had died of a heart attack during the night. Since then, she has dreamed of the Champs-Elysées just twice. Each time, the person she saw in her dream died.

Carberry: "An excellent argument for extrasensory perception, but not for prophetic dreams."

The Dream: In World War II, a United States Army Air Corps officer, based in England, had a recurring dream in which he killed his grandparents. He took his dream to the Mental Hygiene Officer, who asked him just one question: "Are your grandparents alive?" The dreamer replied: "Oh, yes, sir. They're back in the States." The Mental Hygiene Officer told him: "Son, the only people who don't dream of killing their grandparents are people who've never had grandparents to kill in their dreams. All four of *my* grandparents were dead before I was born. Consider yourself lucky and go back to duty." A month later, the dreamer distinguished himself on a bombing mission over a beautiful but strategic German spa. He was awarded several medals, but most rewarding of all: *He never dreamed of killing his grandparents again.* When he returned home, he learned that—back in pre-World War I Germany—his grandmother and grandfather had first met while taking the waters at the very spa that he had destroyed.

Carberry: "If it's a typical dream, as the Mental Hygiene Officer said it was, then the business about the German spa is just a coincidence—the fortunes of war. I'd be interested in knowing more about what became of the Mental Hygiene Officer. . . ."

The Dream: During the California Gold Rush, an experienced and prosperous settler dreamed that some Easterners were trapped in a mountain snowstorm. He awoke, but, when he realized it was just a dream, he went back to sleep—and dreamed the same dream. Since these Easterners were disturbing his sleep, he awoke again and organized a search party. They rescued a band of inexperienced Easterners who actually were marooned a few miles away.

Carberry: "As any history student knows, inexperienced Eastern prospectors—*tenderfeet,* I believe they were called—were all over the map of California in those days. If a search party went ten miles in any direction, I suspect it would have found somebody to rescue."

The Dream: A federal judge dreamed of attending a funeral in a Catholic chapel. During the dream ceremony, the priest pointed at the judge and said, "Thirty-one days!" The judge ignored his dream, but thirty-one days later, he was summoned to a Catholic hospital. His mother had suffered a heart attack. She died there. And the nun who attended her on her death bed had the same face as the priest in the dream!

Carberry: "Nuns don't look like priests."

The Dream: In eighteenth-century England, a young man dreamed of visiting John Milton in Heaven. Milton had been dead for many years and so the young man took the opportunity to tell him how much he liked *Paradise Lost.* Milton beamed and, as they parted, the venerable poet said: "You will do well, too, young man. What is your name?" And the young man replied: "Cowper, sir. William Cowper."

Carberry: "And just *who* was William Cowper?"

The Dream: People occasionally dream of the winner of the next day's horse race.

Carberry: "The same people more often dream of the losers."

I could not let Carberry's last retort go unchallenged. "That's a half-truth," I told him. "If you count all the dreams of racetrack touts, you're probably right. But what about the dreams of people who have absolutely no interest in racing?"

"What about them?" said Carberry.

"Allow me," I said, "to quote your eminent colleague, Professor Dirk Van Huyt, on this subject."

"A wonderful Dutchman!" Carberry exclaimed.

"In his thesis, *Your Prophetic Dreams,* Professor Van Huyt writes:

> Many folks have dreamed the winner of the Derby . . . .
> Fantastically enough, more than half of the dreamers have
> been folk utterly uninterested in the Turf, and knowing the
> name of no racehorses whatever! It is hard to see why such

people have been so favoured in dream, since most of them have not "taken the tip" to such a small degree as to have a modest "bob" on the winner. Yet such "Turf Information" does come true . . . . The "dream horse" certainly seems worth backing. One should put one's *night*shirt on it. . . .

The italics, I might add, are Professor Van Huyt's, not mine."

"Oh, certainly," Carberry declared. "I could almost say I recognize them. He comes across marvelously in translation, doesn't he?"

"Would you care to comment on his findings and advice?"

"Oh, that wily Dutchman! He tells you to bet your nightshirt—but nothing valuable, like money. After all, who has a nightshirt? And, if you do have one, what a wonderful way to get rid of it gracefully! You might even win something—and, even if you don't, you've caught up with modern times by shedding your nightshirt."

I told Carberry that, elsewhere in his thesis, Professor Van Huyt takes a more explicit stand in favor of prophetic dreams: "Your Dutchman says that, in general, dreams predicting a friend's death have great import— particularly if the dream is set in 'a strange, vivid locality which the sleeper has never seen before.' The particular friend who dies in the dream should be warned to take care of himself. And, even if the friend doesn't die, the dreamer owes no apologies—for, as Professor Van Huyt observes, the dream may have served its purpose as a warning of danger."

I expected a sharp counterattack from Carberry, but all that emanated from my sofa was a genteel snore. At almost the same moment, my wife called in heartily from the kitchen: "Soup's on, boys!"

At these words, my guest—who seemed to have dozed off after too many martinis—snapped to attention, pointed a wavering finger at me, and began to talk in a peculiarly intense tone of voice.

"I have just now had a prophetic dream," Carberry said, "that will refute prophetic dreams for all time because it is patently false. I dreamed that I stayed for dinner, that dinner was served, but that I never ate dinner. And yet here we are—about to sit down to dinner. Thus, I contend that if there *are* prophetic dreams, they lie!"

With that, his head tipped over to the side and he fell into a deep sleep. All the king's horses and all the king's men could not have awakened Professor Josiah Carberry until shortly before midnight, when he just barely had time to catch his train.

CHAPTER SIX:

Dreams That Money Can't Buy

Dreams embody the desire not only to see the future, but also to cure the present. This is why bank cashiers dream of faulty ledgers at night and rectify obscure daytime errors in the morning. This is why innocents accused of crimes often manage to dream up witnesses and alibis which, on occasion, stand up in court. There are dreams that heal. There are dreams that prove more effective than whole shelves of self-improvement manuals.

In the last two chapters, I have discussed dreams that may have altered history and dreams that—over my friend Carberry's half-dead body—definitely have anticipated history. They were dreamed, for the most part, by famous people or about them.

I come now to dreams by dreamers of whom you may never have heard, but some of whose situations are very similar to your own. These dreams have seldom affected the world we live in, but they have solved a man's pressing problem or made a downtrodden woman's life a little more bearable. In a society that observes National Letter Writing Week and National Allergy Month every year, it is altogether fitting and proper that we pause to pay tribute to the every-night dreams of everyday people.

Science tells us that people who dream about their problems often dream up solutions at the same time. Unfortunately, as memory fades, solutions are the first to go.

But dreams can provide your first glimpse of a problem. Your best friend may be having an escapade with your spouse, but you would be the last to know because you are, after all, married to one and trusting in both. In dreams, however, the truth may prove inescapable.

That is your problem, not your solution—for the evidence of dreams is not grounds for divorce in any state of the Union at this time.

Still, if a solution exists and it has eluded us in waking life, it is worth searching for in dream life. In dreams, we tend to ignore false clues, commercial pressures, and sheer expediency—the trees that render us unable to see the forest.

The healing, improving, and problem-solving dreams that you will encounter here loomed large in the lives of people who had—as who hasn't!—an infinite variety of complaints. Neither their problems nor their solutions would make headlines anywhere but on these pages. All in all, however, they comprise an astonishing testimonial to what dreams can do for *you!*

CURED SELF OF WIFE!

A Dutch widower was courting a merry widow, but every time he stood on the brink of proposing, a vision of his late lamented wife would appear before him and freeze his words of love in mid-gurgle.

The hitherto merry widow grew restless and surly. "You have exactly twenty-four hours to make me an offer," she told the starry-eyed but tongue-tied Dutchman. "Otherwise I will go to Paris and play the field."

The thought of his merry widow in a French lover's arms gave the Dutchman pangs of jealousy and heartburn, and so he tried again to propose. Once more, the vision of his late wife paralyzed him.

That night, the Dutchman told his troubles to an old friend—a bachelor tulip merchant from Amsterdam. "Alas," the inconsolable widower concluded, "nothing will ever grow in my garden of love."

His bachelor friend patted him on the shoulder and said: "There, there, my dear boy. Do you truly love this—*woman*?"

"Hopelessly."

"Then rejoice, you hard-headed but adorable Dutchman. Because we are such true friends, I will give you my Leyden Papyrus."

"A sheet of paper from Leyden?"

"Yes, but one that is specially impregnated."

"And what do I do with it? Make my will on it? Write my suicide note?"

"No, silly boy," his friend said. "You write a letter on it to your dead wife. You list all the good things you have done for her in your lifetime. Then you simply insist that she go away."

"Maybe I need two sheets to list all the good things I did for her?"

"If so, you write on both sides of your Leyden Papyrus. When you sit down and think about it, though, you'll probably find trouble filling one side of it. Anyway, I have only one."

That night, the widower filled out his Leyden Papyrus and tied it to his wrist when he went to bed. In his second dream of the night, his dead wife appeared—right on schedule. He served her with a summons shaped like the rolled-up parchment on his wrist. She went away forever.

Although this solved his problem, his story did not have a totally happy ending. When he went to propose to his merry widow, he found that she had already left for Paris. He never saw her again. That is the happy part, for the widower got over the merry widow, who was not right for him anyway. But now he misses his dead wife.

Improved His English in One Easy Vision!

A Frenchman, studying English, dreamed he met Sir Laurence Olivier and told him: "I called to you yesterday, but you were out of town."

"Nonsense," Sir Laurence replied with classical hauteur. "You speak English like a coxcomb. You should say that you called *on* me."

When the Frenchman awoke, his dream remained so vivid that he consulted a textbook and found that Sir Laurence was absolutely correct.

DECIPHERED LOVE LETTER!

Ever since her high-school days, a fast-rising New York fashion model has had a crush on her Home Economics teacher—a husky combat veteran of World War II.

She lost contact with him for many years. Soon after a particularly gaunt-looking picture of her appeared on the cover of a popular women's magazine, she received a letter from him. He reported his joy at discovering a former pupil on the cover of his favorite periodical, but alarm at seeing her so cadaverously thin. "Surely," he wrote, "you can find someone to cook for you."

She was so touched by his concern for her that tears of genuine emotion—her first, she recalled, in two years and eleven months—fell from her eyes and blurred the closing words of the letter beyond recognition.

That night, she dreamed that the missing words were: "Will you marry me?"

In the middle of the night, she called her former teacher at home and announced: "The answer is yes!" He seemed a trifle perplexed, but at her request he flew with her to Mexico. There he obtained a quickie divorce from his wife, who has yet to recover from the sudden end of her marriage. "We were quite happy," she says over and over. "We had two children and were planning a third."

The Home Economics teacher married his former pupil in Acapulco. When he returned to work, the Parent-Teacher Association protested so vigorously that he lost his job. His new wife, however, earns more than enough to support him and even pay his alimony.

GOT RICH QUICK!

A Texas farmer, whose Government surplus money had been suspended pending an investigation, needed cash in a hurry. He dreamed that there was oil somewhere on his 3,000-acre farm. But he didn't have enough funds to make tests. In a later dream, however, the location was pinpointed. He is now a wealthy Texan even among Texans.

Mastered Russian in Sleep!

Miss Elinor Silverman of New York City tends to run hours late when she is busy. She once showed up toward midnight at a home to which she had been invited for 8 P.M.

Her hostess, an American of Russian descent, apparently had given up on Miss Silverman's ever coming. She had, in fact, retired for the night.

When Miss Silverman rang the downstairs buzzer, she was astonished to hear—over the Intercom—her hostess cursing her in fluent Russian.

Arriving upstairs, Miss Silverman found that her hostess had gone back to sleep. Miss Silverman awakened her again and told her what she had just heard.

"Nonsense," said the hostess. "I heard Russian spoken in my parents' home, but I never learned it myself." She also told Miss Silverman to help herself to anything in the ice box, but please to let her sleep in peace.

Miss Silverman was unable to put her mind at ease. By ringing her hostess' buzzer at odd hours on various nights, she soon ascertained that her former friend had indeed developed an extensive vocabulary of Russian folk wisdom and profanity—but only while asleep. Miss Silverman then took her findings to a respected, but overly pompous, dream interpreter for analysis.

"You have nothing to worry about," he assured her. "Your friend has a simple case of *xenoglossia.*"

"Please, doctor, what is *xenoglossia* and is it curable? Miss Silverman pleaded.

"You needn't call me doctor," he said modestly. "And *xenoglossia* is a very benign form of *glossolalia.*"

Miss Silverman was now perilously close to hysteria. For reassurance, the dream interpreter referred her to Havelock Ellis' *The World of Dreams:*

Speaking in a language not consciously known, or *xenoglossia* as it is now termed, occurs under various abnormal conditions, as well as in sleep, and is sometimes classed with the tendency which is found, especially under great religious excitement, to "speak with tongues" or to utter gibberish.

He then began to explain *glossolalia,* of which *xenoglossia* is merely a minor sub-category, but Miss Silverman left hurriedly. She remarked that she would rather be cursed in Russian than badgered by gibberish.

ENGAGED NAKED AMAZON FOR ART'S SAKE!

There is a Greenwich Village sculptor who is better known to police blotters than to art critics. He has been involved in so many paternity suits that no self-respecting model will pose for him—even with clothes on.

His shortage of models threatened to end his career as a sculptor until he began dreaming of an unclothed woman. She is sixty feet tall and perfectly proportioned. Every morning and early afternoon, while he sleeps, she comes into his dream and poses magnificently. Every afternoon, during his two working hours, he reproduces part of his dream. He is calling it "Bigger Than Life Study #1."

Thanks to a few items in gossip columns, several international art collectors have approached the sculptor, but he says that his "Bigger Than Life Study #1" is not for sale. His sudden withdrawal from previous habits seems, however, to have created a market for his earlier, hitherto unacclaimed, sculptures.

SOLVED CRIME!

In 1827, Maria Marten of Polstead, England, ran off with William Corder, a farmer whose intentions were not the best. In fact, they were the very worst. Corder reneged on his solemn promise to marry Maria. Adding injury to insult, he murdered her. He buried her under the floor of a red barn.

Corder then made a fatal mistake: He wrote to Maria's parents that all was well.

Maria's mother brooded over Corder's letter for almost a year. It did not quite ring true! One night, she dreamed that she witnessed Maria's murder and furtive burial.

After Mrs. Marten had nagged her husband sufficiently, he visited the only red barn in the vicinity. By demolishing its floor, he discovered his daughter's body in a burlap bag. Her corpse was in dreadful condition, which belied Corder's reassuring letter. A dentist had to make positive identification.

Their suspicions aroused by this discovery, British police interrogated Corder, who had married and moved to Essex. Confronted by Mrs. Marten's dream and Miss Marten's corpse, he confessed. He was executed in August, 1828.

SAVED LIVES!

These dreams abound—particularly in wartime. A seaman dreams he is attacked by a shark; his commander heeds the omen and finds an enemy submarine. . . . A platoon leader dreams of a mine field and leads most of his men safely through it the next day. . . .

On Mother's Day, 1962, a Midwestern woman dreamed that her only son was in great danger. She wrote him an urgent letter and sent it air mail to him in Saigon, where he was on Army duty as a technical adviser to the Vietnamese forces.

The letter reached him just as he was about to embark upon an illicit helicopter jaunt with a Vietnamese peasant who had promised to show him the countryside in all its spring splendor. The American youth cancelled his journey. Soon after, the peasant was unmasked as a Vietcong guerrilla. The young man insists that he owes his life to the dream of his mother, a humble woman who concedes that she still cannot pinpoint Saigon on a map of Asia.

MADE FILM HISTORY!

Film editors Radley H. Metzger and Bill Kyriakys had invested some $35,000 of their life savings—plus countless hours of time and talent—in making their own independent film, *Dark Odyssey*, about a Greek sailor stalking a family enemy in New York City. Film distributors turned down their film because it lacked "name" actors and nudity.

The two moviemakers had virtually abandoned hope when, one night, Metzger had his usual recurring dream —in which he delivers his motion-picture camera to the Most Beautiful Woman in the World. This time, however, the Most Beautiful Woman in the World thanked Metzger *in Greek*.

Metzger and Kyriakys dubbed their film's sound track into Greek and got a booking at a foreign-language film house near Times Square. *Dark Odyssey* was cordially reviewed by the New York *Times* and other newspapers. As a result of the interest created by the Greek version, the English-language version soon went into national release under the title of *Passionate Sunday*.

WROTE BEST-SELLERS!

"Mrs. Radcliffe, the novelist of horror, took to eating the most indigestible foods in order to procure nightmares for insertion in her tales of horror and mystery. Dryden similarly ate raw flesh to promote dreams of luxurious splendor," one historian writes.

Storm Jameson, a British authoress, often dreams of unknown gardens with white flowers after a hard day that has ended in frustration. She awakens with new ideas, new solutions, and occasionally a fresh variation on a familiar plot.

RESISTED COMPROMISE!

Meyer Levin, the author of *Compulsion*, was asked by the publisher of an earlier book, *Citizens*, to change his principal character from a Jew to a Swede. *Levin made the change, but then he dreamed of having a lion and a tiger on leashes. The two animals had grown up together, but now they were quarreling and threatening to tear Levin apart in their ferocious struggle. He considered giving up one of the animals, but he valued both and decided to manage with both.*

Upon awakening, Levin realized the dream's significance: "The tiger and the lion were my Jewish heritage and my talent; in each was my strength, and now I feared that they would destroy each other and destroy me, but I couldn't sell them, I couldn't part with them, I had to find a way for them to live together."

Levin notified his publisher that he could not make the change. *Citizens* was published without compromise. Critics ranked it with *The Grapes of Wrath* and other fine novels of the time.

COMPOSED GLORIOUS MUSIC!

The French composer, Camille Saint-Saëns, was on Army maneuvers. Military life swelled his appetite and, after eating heartily one night, he presented his compliments to the chef.

"And what, may I ask, is the name of the unique and flavorsome main dish I have just eaten?" Saint-Saëns asked the mess sergeant.

"Horse stew," the man replied with Gallic directness.

That night, the composer was afflicted by unpleasant dreams accompanied by mournful music.

"I shall never eat horse stew again," he vowed. He kept his word.

Many years later, he needed some opening bars for a "Requiem Mass" he was composing. Remembering the music that had accompanied his post-horsemeat dreams, he incorporated it into his composition. Thus, there is beauty even in horsemeat.

All of the examples cited in this chapter have been dreams that money cannot buy. It might even be said that the best dreams in life are free.

In recent years, however, the money-changers have gained admission to our innermost citadels of dreams. Through tape recordings placed beneath pillows or played through loudspeakers, sleepers can now (or will soon be able to) learn to speak fluent Serbo-Croatian, give up nail-biting, solve chess problems, take salesmanship courses, and even listen to Dr. Norman Vincent Peale. All projections indicate that "sleep learning"—as it is called—will be a $50,000,000-a-year industry in 1984.

CHAPTER SEVEN:

How To Interpret Your Dreams

"Little manuals on the interpretation of dreams have been much valued by the uncultured classes," Havelock Ellis wrote rather patronizingly. He may have had in mind such British chapbooks (equivalents of America's "Little Blue Books," but sold primarily by peddlers) as one with the intriguing title of *Dreams and Moles with Their Interpretation and Signification Made Far More Manifest and Plain than any Published to the Very Meanest Capacities by the Most Ancient as Well as the Most Modern Rules of Philosophy*.

In America, dream literature began under more reputable auspices. The first manual was published in 1795 in Portsmouth, New Hampshire, and incorporated in the *Book of Knowledge*—hardly a title calculated to woo the uncultured classes. It contained such wisdom as: "To dream of washing denotes an easement from pain or troubles."

Subsequently, the field has declined in quality, but not in quantity. Anyone who has ever patrolled the pornography parlors within a two-block radius of Times Square will know that there is no shortage of dream books—most of them quite innocent and valuable only to the smut merchant's pretensions of respectability. The data in these volumes is, to say the least, unrevealing: "Dreaming of fleas denotes disquiet." . . . "To dream that you have hog's bristles signifies great and violent danger." . . . "To dream you see a person hanging on a gibbet is a sign of damage."

Even if these interpretations are accurate, how many of us actually dream of fleas or hog bristles? What layman knows that a gibbet is a form of gallows? Until I looked it up in a dictionary, I had presumed it was an edible part of a chicken.

Some of the dream books go by opposites. Poverty betokens money to come. Friends mean you will make enemies. Black means white and white means black. By this logic, the best dream of all is that you are wallowing in mud up to your neck, which is broken.

The best dream books of all are Freud, Havelock Ellis, *Rip Van Winkle*, and the *Bible* with its tales of dreams by Daniel, Gideon, Nebuchadnezzar, among others. With the exception of the *Bible*, however, few of these are readily available on the mass market.

The inadequacies of available dream books inspired me to confine my research to some 200 common dreams, but to treat each with the respect it deserved. Where there was controversy over a dream's implications, I presented both sides. Where I felt strongly that a particular interpretation was meaningful, I said so. Where I had my own special insights or experiences to offer, I declined to cloak them in false modesty. My findings will be set forth in depth a chapter hence.

But, even before I had distilled the dream interpretations of many centuries, I sensed a shortcoming that afflicts even the best dream books: a lack of brass-tacks advice on such fundamentals as *how to* record your dreams and *how to* go about interpreting them. Should you keep a pad by your bedside, trust to memory, or awaken your bedmate? What questions should you ask yourself? What traps must be avoided? How can you relate an abstract dream to concrete experience? These and other vital practicalities have been glossed over or ignored by experts and quacks alike.

I sought the advice of three veteran dreamers of the past—Michel Eyquem de Montaigne, Benjamin Franklin, and Miss Anna Eva Fay.

Montaigne, the best-known essayist of sixteenth-century France, wrote: "I believe it to be true that dreams are the true interpreters of our inclinations, but there is an art required to sort and understand them." Montaigne's words were not merely directed at sixteenth-century dreamers; he was truly a man for all seasons.

Franklin, in an essay on "The Art of Procuring Pleasant Dreams," wrote that if you prepare properly for sleep—by not eating or drinking too much, by getting plenty of fresh air and exercise, and by sleeping in a comfortable bed—you will have useful dreams worthy of daytime contemplation.

Anna Eva Fay needs no introduction to devotees of dream interpretation. She was a turn-of-the-century dream analyst, stage performer and theosophist. (A theosophist is someone who believes he or she has a direct line to God via mystical insight, philosophical speculation or direct distance dialing.) Since she also interpreted dreams by mail, Miss Fay had as many as five secretaries assisting her at her headquarters in Melrose Highlands, Massachusetts.

Just before dropping off to sleep at the end of a hard day, Miss Fay would induce important dreams of her own by recalling one particularly delightful experience—a trip to the Passion Play at Oberammergau, Germany. "In such sleep as follows," she said, "I see people and conditions that show me my present mistakes and how to avoid them in the future and I see paths to tread of which I should have been in ignorance."

While many of her endeavors appear to have had their commercial side, Miss Fay stressed their spiritual worth. She even dedicated an anthology of her dream interpretations with these words of militant piety:

> To the Public: I would rather be a Hottentot and dwell in the wilds of Africa than to betray a human Christ and be a Judas.

We shall hear more of Anna Eva Fay at several places in the next chapter—including the category of *dreams of Almonds*.

Some of my sources contained excellent examples of *how not to* interpret dreams.

Havelock Ellis, for instance, dreamed himself into the plaza of a Spanish city. The Governor emerged from his palace and spoke to his subordinates in flawless English.

Ellis pondered the symbolism of a Spanish Governor addressing Spaniards in a language other than Spanish. Was the Governor a British spy? Was a war between Spain and England imminent? Or was the Governor telling State secrets that he did not wish the populace to overhear?

After much analysis, Ellis determined why the Governor spoke English: The dreamer was an Englishman, not a Spaniard. Most people dream in their native tongues.

Ellis wasted too much of his time over the language rather than its content, but he did not waste ours. From his experience, we can learn this vital lesson: *Disregard false clues.*

Sigmund Freud had another tidbit of advice: "The apparently innocent dreams turn out to be quite the reverse when we take the trouble to analyze them. They are, if I may say so, wolves in sheep's clothing."

Particularly if you wade into the dreams of others, you must always be prepared to get far more than your feet wet. You may penetrate layers that are best left untouched.

Freud once had such an experience. A noted lawyer—who was not a patient of Freud's—told him casually:

"I dream that I am walking in front of my house with a lady on my arm. A closed carriage is standing there, waiting. A man steps up to me, shows me his credentials as a police officer, and asks me to follow him. I ask only for time in which to arrange my affairs. What do you make of that, Freud? Can it be that I—a pillar of the community and an ex-officio leader of the Vienna Bar Association—wish to get arrested?"

"Certainly not," Freud conceded. "But do you happen to know on what charge you were arrested?"

"Infanticide."

"The murder of your new-born child? Horrible! Horrible! But, if I know my criminal law, only a *mother* can be convicted of infanticide. If anyone else does it, the crime is just another homicide."

"True, Freud, true. But that is the way I dreamed it."

"And you a lawyer," Freud observed with a sedate cluck. "Under what circumstances did you dream this dream? What happened the evening before?"

"Hmmm, if you don't mind, Freud, I'd rather not say. A rather delicate matter, if you know what I mean."

"I need to know. Otherwise, no dream interpretation. . . ."

"Well, then. If I must tell you, it is in strict confidence. I spent the night not at home, but in the bed of a lady who means a great deal to me."

"Ah, your charming wife!"

"No, Freud. I must confess that I spent the night in the bed of another woman."

"And the woman was there, too?"

"Precisely. You see, we are very passionate with each other. In fact, we were passionate thrice last night before we drifted off to sleep. And, when we awoke before breakfast, our passion renewed itself—if you know what I mean. Then I fell asleep again and had the dream I just told you."

"This passionate woman is married?"

"Yes."

"And you do not wish her to conceive?"

"Certainly not, Freud. That would expose us. I would have to resign from the bar association."

"Then you do not practice normal sexual intercourse?"

"Well, man to man, let us just say that I take the precaution of bowing out an instant before there might be any lasting complications."

"Am I to assume that you took this precaution thrice last night and once this morning? If so, I suspect that you are not quite sure you succeeded in withdrawing at the proper time."

"That might be so, Freud. But you make it sound so damn mechanical."

"Your dream, my friend," Freud said triumphantly,

"is indeed the fulfillment of a wish: By this dream you are assured that you have not begotten an unwanted child or—what amounts to the same thing—that you have killed the child."

The lawyer praised Freud's discernment, but the good doctor had not finished. "The mention of infanticide has yet to be explained," Freud continued.

"Oh, never mind that, Freud. You've done just fine. After all, it was you who asked the question that brought up the whole bloody matter of infanticide."

"I find your behavior quite fascinating—clinically speaking," Freud remarked dryly. "And I also wonder why this crime, which is peculiar to deranged females, occurs to *you*."

"Well, Freud, if it will help you in any way, I will fill in a few more embarrassing details. Years ago, as a struggling young law clerk, I got a barmaid in the family way. She knew that I didn't want to marry her or father her child, so she went ahead and had an abortion without even telling me until it was all over. Perhaps now you can comprehend a little of the guilt I feel."

"Now I understand," Freud remarked gently. The philandering lawyer lived to regret having bared his *amours*. While Freud did not gossip about the man or his escapades, he often used the dream and its background in his books and lectures. The lawyer's fear that his case history was recognizable caused him to shun bar association meetings and social events, although he did not alter his bedroom habits one whit.

In discussing what *not* to do, I would append this advice to the horrible examples aready cited: *Do not try to interpret every dream*. Some dreams are as fleeting as weather reports. They are obsolete by the time you awaken. Freud himself said: "The question whether every dream can be interpreted is to be answered in the negative."

The dream to capture is the recurring dream—or, at least, any dream that substantially repeats itself at least three or four times a month. It is not until you have studied your dreams for at least a month that you can hope to extract dream symbols that may ultimately prove meaningful.

In evaluating a dream, do not remain oblivious to external circumstances and personal identities. A dream of fleas may be insignificant, but not if you are a dog. A dream of gallows may seem remote, but not if you are a condemned man.

One anthropologist reported a woman's dream of dark, boxlike canyon passages. Sigmund Freud might have had a field day with this as a pure erotic fantasy. But the dreamer was a Hopi Indian who used to live near Grand Canyon in constant fear that her little son might fall into the abyss. . . .

With all these *don'ts* dogging your footsteps, you come now to the ten basic steps toward interpreting your own dreams:

1. Before retiring at night, place a ruled pad or notebook at bedside. Unlined scratch pads may be more economical, but you will have enough difficulty deciphering your early-morning handwriting without having to wonder in which direction it is headed.

Pencil notes can be illegible. Keep a pen at bedside. If it is an ink pen, unsheath it and check the ink supply. If a ball-point pen, examine the ink supply; piggyback refills are preferable. This may sound trivial now, but I know of at least one suicide attempt that was contemplated after a befuddled dreamer had scrawled copious notes with an empty pen. Fortunately, the fatal solution was rejected because, without ink, the frustrated man was equally incapable of composing a suicide note.

If at all possible, keep a lamp within easy reach. Make a mental note of its location before turning it off.

If you sleep in a double bed, it is even better to have a narrow-beam bed light that will not illuminate your bed partner. Many sleepers have set out to record their dreams and ended up in all-night wrangles with their bedmates. It is advisable beforehand to warn your spouse—or whoever else is sharing your bed—to disregard scratching noises.

As a final measure before Lights Out, place a pitcher of water (preferably iced) at bedside. Should you have a dream of thirst and then awaken, the water will prove invaluable.

2. After turning off the light, say softly to yourself: "A dream uninterpreted is like a letter unopened. I will not trust to memory. I will write down all that I dream." Repeat this catchy vow seven times.

Then, in similar fashion, tell yourself: "Upon awakening to record each dream, I will guard my fine edge of sleep. Insomnia is the enemy of all good dreams." You need repeat this admonition only thrice.

Finally, speak the first admonition ("A dream uninterpreted. . . .", etc.) once more—and approximately every two-and-a-half minutes thereafter until you are fast asleep.

3. Immediately after each dream, awaken. *This is important.*

Then record every detail of your dream—no matter how negligible it may appear in the small hours.

Avoid looking at your alarm clock or watch, for in awareness of time there is a dangerous link with the conscious world.

If you are thirsty, sip water, but do not leave your bed.

If you have turned on the lamp, turn it off before returning to sleep.

Repeat this procedure after each dream.

Do not smoke in bed.

4. Upon awakening in the morning and before eating breakfast or even brushing your teeth: Write a summary of all your dreams for the night—*without consulting your nocturnal jottings*. Try to recall all details.

You are now free to eat breakfast and clean your teeth, in whichever order you prefer.

Over breakfast, compare your two sets of notes. Observe all discrepancies between your dream-by-dream jottings (which will be referred to henceforth as *List A*) and your morning-after summary (*List B*).

5. During the waking day—while at work, at lunch, or en route—jot down any additional recollections of your

night's dreaming and try to associate them with the events of the preceding day. These additional jottings are *List C*.

6. Before dinner, compare Lists A, B, and C. How well do they jibe? On what points do they contradict each other? Which one or two symbols or settings seem to stand out?

Note the salient differences on a fourth list—*List D*.

7. After dinner, make a list of your current wishes—however vague, impractical, idealistic, or anti-social they may be. *This is List E.*

Make a separate file or folder for each of your lists. Perform Steps 1 through 7 diligently every day and night for a full week.

8. At the end of each week, review Lists A through D (ignore List E for a while) and begin a new roster —*List F*. Break your dreams down into components such as feelings, objects, settings, actions, and words of dialogue that occurred during your seven nights of dreaming. Underline any components that recur.

Examine the underlined items in your List F. Look for any that seem related to each other. Try to link them by such means as the all-inclusive generality (for example, dreaming of *cutting off your nose to spite your face, getting castrated,* and *paying income tax* can all be lumped under "AMPUTATION"), the far-fetched pun (tardy mother = MARMALADE), or free association. Many amateur interpreters refer to Step 8 as the "fun phase" or "creative play period."

Destroy Lists A through D.

Perform Step 8 once a week for four to six weeks.

9. You will now have four to six Lists F. Compile their recurring symbols in one last roster—*List G.*

Destroy all your Lists F.

10. Dig out your bulging file of Lists E—the daily collection of your current wishes—and compare with your List G. Make any free associations that jump to mind. What do your wishes and your dreams tell you about yourself?

The comparison of Lists E and G will tell you the obvious answers. But on List G will be many items that seem to bare no relation to the wishes on List E.

You are now ready to look up these unaffiliated symbols from List G. You should hope to find many of them in the next chapter. What clues do they give to your wishes? What do they tell you about your past? Wherever possible, I have sought to apply the wisdom of ancient dream interpreters to current situations. Do not underrate the dream logic of centuries past. For what's past, as Shakespeare said, is prologue. . . .

CHAPTER EIGHT:

Abortion to Zebra:
The 200 Most Common Dreams
And What They Mean

ABORTION—To dream of the sin of criminal abortion is an omen that your health is in danger. Also, guard your loved ones during the period of stress that will ensue. If an unmarried woman is afflicted by this dream, she will be maligned by gossip. Take every precaution.

ABROAD—If you dream of foreign travel, you are likely to change your vocation in the near future. . . . Even if you do not change jobs, you are likely to take a trip. In any event, your life will enter an unsettled phase, however brief. . . . Should a mature woman dream of foreign travel, she will either make a journey or undergo change of life before long. Should a bachelor dream of foreign travel, he is likely to fall in love with a woman of a different religion. If his parents are living, they will most certainly make trouble. . . . No matter who you are: If you have this dream, be receptive to interviews, invitations, propositions, recruiters, strangers, blind dates, and bolts from the blue.

ADULTERY—Should you dream that you have violated the Seventh Commandment, you may anticipate more than your customary quota of troubles in the weeks ahead. To dream, however, that you have successfully resisted fornication portends great danger culminating happily in victory or escape. If you are in love and dream that you have overcome this immoral urge, now is the time to pursue the object of your affections

—unless he or she be married to another. If, in any adultery dream, you see yourself black-skinned, you will be caught in the act of adultery—unless you already be a Negro, in which case you can disregard the racial aspect. If you dream of adultery, the best you can hope for is a mild illness. Avoid private detectives.

AEROPLANE—see AIRPLANE.

AIRPLANE—see PLANE.

ALMONDS—Even in chocolate bars, almonds are controversial. Some like them; some don't. In dreams as in life, almonds are the kernels of dispute. In her *Somnolency and Guide to Dreams,* Anna Eva Fay intones ominously: "To dream one sees or eats almonds signifies difficulties and troubles." On the other hand, Leo Francis, in *Dreams and their Meaning,* observes jauntily: "If you are eating and enjoying almonds, it is a good sign." I lean toward the pessimistic theory, particularly if the almonds of your dream taste bitter. Sweet, tasty almonds are more likely to portend some enjoyment and perhaps travel, but you will spare yourself worry if you never dream of almonds.

AMPUTATION—To dream that one's head was removed used to be a bad omen in ancient Greece—unless the dreamer had the good fortune of being a prisoner on trial for a capital offense. In such a case, a dream of beheading was all to the good, because the Law of Double Jeopardy prohibited any person's being beheaded twice. . . . Even today, to dream that one's nose is cut off implies loss of life, liberty, or—even worse—prestige in the community. Perfume salesmen can thwart destiny by changing jobs (even at financial sacrifice) after recurrent loss-of-nose dreams. . . . Anyone else who dreams of amputation should think twice before taking a trip, particularly on a disreputable airline.

ANGELS—Deal discreetly with angels. Seeing them in

a dream means good news, unless you also talk with them—in which case you proceed at your own risk. But, if you hold your tongue with angels, you may perchance receive a legacy, a bequest, a prize, or a tax refund. If a pregnant woman dreams of two angels, she will be delivered of twins; three angels, triplets, etc. History hints that a nineteenth century housewife in old Bangkok dreamed of two angels performing a sinuous exotic dance on the head of one pin. The next morning she gave birth to Siamese twins. As a rule of thumb, it is foolish to rush in where angels fear to tread.

APES—To dream of apes is not good, according to Old Aunt Dinah. Other authorities are less definite; the consensus is that it depends on what the apes are doing.

APPLES—To dream of apples that are sweet, ripe, and juicy betokens fertility to virgins and success to those who covet virgins. If you fit into neither category, you may still anticipate success in one or more of the following: business, love, marriage, longevity, parenthood. Ever since Eve—of Biblical fame—sour apples have signified contention, sedition, eviction, vice, and Original Sin. . . . To dream of whole orchards of apples implies good news by the bushel. . . . One dream interpreter recalls an unusual experience: "My wife was pregnant and I dreamed of eating an apple. It was in the First World Brawl, and the fruit had not been seen around for some weeks. I happened to tell her of my dream and she answered: 'I've been dying for an apple for days and days, but wouldn't tell you because I knew you'd go to a lot of trouble for nothing.'" The dream interpreter's conclusion proved even more remarkable: "Pregnant women get strange food fancies. . . . It is all associated with fertility."

APPOINTMENT—Dreams of missing appointments, missing trains, and all other inhibited movement were classified by Freud as *Dreams of Paralysis*. Freud gave this example: "One tries to move forward, but finds one-self glued to the spot. One tries to reach something but is held up by a series of obstacles. . . . One raises one's hand to avenge an insult, but finds it powerless." Freud considered these, in part, attempts to overcome the fear of death. He also decided that they involved inhibition of the sexual impulse but, as we have already seen in Chapter Seven, Freud was practically a zealot about coitus interruptus. . . . Dream interpreters who are less Freudian than Freud—as who isn't?—concede that such dreams of paralysis represent a conflict between two wishes. It is perhaps summed up in the vernacular of Mr. James Durante, who once inquired: "Did you ever get the feeling that you wanted to stay and then you got the feeling that you wanted to go?" In your dream, one wish may prove stronger than the other. After such a dream, it is important to break it down into two wish-components and note which part won. . . . *Still other interpretations of varying merit*: Fear of missing an opportunity . . . your last chance . . . awareness of a vast gap in age between you and one you love . . . chronic lateness.

AROUSE—To dream that you disturb, arouse, or awaken somebody else is a good dream. To dream that you awaken from a dream is a natural epilogue of the phenomenon known to Science as "a dream within a dream." Very often, particularly when you are involved in interpreting dreams, you will dream that you awaken and tell someone your dream. To the serious-minded interpreter of one's own dreams, this is the ultimate Dream of Convenience. It enables you to make a record of your dream and still go on sleeping. Unfortunately, such records prove useless in the morning. But they do indicate that you sleep cleverly.

ARTICHOKE—To dream of this delectable thistle or its edible tubers promises succor galore. Whoever dreams of artichokes can face the future serenely.

ASS—If you see a jackass, your affairs—particularly those of the heart—will go well indeed. But if you ride a jackass in your dream, you are headed for a senseless quarrel. If you are walking behind a jackass atop a precipice, you will fall into deep trouble—as will anyone who allows a donkey to guide his path through life. If you dream that you are walking in front of a donkey or a mule, beware of sudden thrusts of fate. To dream that one of these phlegmatic creatures is chasing you implies that slander will dog your trail—but have no fear, for the poisoned tongue invariable poisons the poisoner. With these exceptions, virtually any dream of donkeys is worth having. The donkey is a symbol of patience, fortitude in the bearing of burdens, and longevity. As one dream interpreter has observed astutely: "Nobody has ever seen a dead donkey." To which Professor Dirk Van Huyt recently added: "Nor a thin donkey." Thus, a dream of donkeys indicates that you will never lack for physical comfort. It also tells you that you are a better listener than a talker, so keep your ears pricked. . . . For a marriage-minded young woman to have such a dream means the mate that fate has her intended for will be amiable but not wealthy, stubborn but not insufferably proud.

B

BABY—The baby signifies truth itself. Therefore, heed any dream involving a baby. If the baby is healthy and happy, you will thrive as a lover, a charmer, a seducer, a salesman, or in whatever direction you choose to turn your talents. But, if the baby is sick or sad, beware of illness, death, or other sorrows in your immediate family. . . . If an unmarried woman dreams of having a baby, she should avoid erotic temptation for several days. If a man dreams of giving birth to a baby, his masculinity will be questioned. . . . Baby dreams should always be interpreted with an eye for symbolism. Thus, if you dream that you receive a baby that is newly severed from the umbilical cord, avoid all gifts—for they will have strings attached. . . . One dream interpreter claims: "Every baby is another embodiment of the Christ Child and if it soon sheds its divinity, that is by human frailty. The dream of the baby is promise of enrichment of the whole world and in particular of your own tiny sphere. It is an intimation to 'set your house in order,' to sweep and dust the untidy corners of your mind."

BACON—If you dream of eating bacon or other pork products all by yourself, the fat is truly in the fire. Someone you know will die. If not, your own health will suffer, your worries will multiply, your love life will sicken, and your enemies will flourish. The Orthodox Jews were among the first to comprehend the evils of bacon. Latterday dream interpreters have denounced bacon vehemently, although a blushing few tolerate it privately with their eggs. The best that any reputable dream interpreter will say publicly is this: "If you dream you are eating bacon in mixed company, nothing too dreadful will happen to you."

BATS—To dream of bats is most inauspicious.

BATHING—To dream of taking a bath is an unpropitious omen for small, dirty boys. It does not augur well for others, either. Resign yourself to hardship. If the bath water is clean, you will survive your ordeal and perhaps even gain from it. If the water is dirty, you will suffer meaninglessly. If the water is hot, your family will give you trouble. If the water is cold, total strangers will give you trouble. If it is dirty and tepid, everybody hates you.

BEANS—To dream of beans signifies minor disturbances, perhaps gastric. If you are in love, brace yourself for a lover's quarrel. If you are in transit, allow for delays; arrange lengthy stopovers. If you are in uniform, make sure you lock your foot locker before leaving. Dreams of beans are never particularly ominous unless

they involve bean-and-~~bacon~~ soup. . . . To dream that
you are climbing a beanstalk implies that you will make
"~~plenty of jack~~" —a slang euphemism for money and a
classic example of punning in dreams.

BEDBUGS—"To dream of these filthy vermin is a sure
indication of sickness and of many enemies seeking to
injure you," says *Everybody's Dream Book,* which is not
my favorite bedside reading. . . . Bedbugs are a threat
to both dreaming and dream interpretation. The case of
a highly respected citizen of Shippingport, Kentucky,
bears repetition. Whenever he dreamed of visiting Indianapolis, he would awaken with small but painful
bites all over his body. At his wife's behest, he consulted a nearby dream analyst. The dreamer was urged
to visit Indianapolis and track down the source of his
scabrous welts. He refused with what seemed at the
time to be undue vehemence. Not long after, he died of
apoplexy. Only when his will was contested did his
neighbors in Shippingport learn that he had a mistress
and a small son living in a bedbug-infested hovel on the
outskirts of Indianapolis.

BEE—To dream that bees, wasps or hornets sting you
shows that you will associate with people who will talk
against you and perhaps actively seek to discredit you.
If you are criminally assaulted, they will whisper that
you either wanted it or provoked it. Guard your good
name as best you can! . . . If the bees do not sting, the
gossip will be about others. Do not be caught up in it or
you will emerge a victim. . . . If you dream that bees
have nested on your property and are making honey
there, you will prosper. If you are a seasoned investor,
consider wax stocks. . . . A number of dream interpreters
are also rabid beekeepers; it is one of the favorite
hobbies in our profession. Perhaps this is why one of
them takes a particularly Utopian view of bee dreams:
"You will not be permitted to be a useless drone. You will
earn a comfortable living, but must be careful to ac-
cummulate a 'store' against rainy days. Your love experi-

ence will be thrilling, but turbulent and brief. The mellowing of a long marriage is not for you. If you are a woman, your spouse will be fickle. But that will teach him to be more than ordinarily chivalrous to you." . . . If you should dream of birds and bees in tandem, none of the above is relevant. Regardless of your age or inclinations, you are simply undergoing an adolescent sex fantasy.

BEER—To dream you are drinking beer portends disappointment. If you are a minor, you will be rebuffed in a tavern. To dream that you are brewing malt into beer, however, is a good omen. If an unmarried girl dreams that she is drinking beer, she will marry an alcoholic. If a married woman dreams that she is drinking beer, her next child will not be a beautiful baby. To dream of Miss Rheingold is delightful.

BLOOD—If a poor man dreams that he vomits blood of a good color, he will receive unexpected cash. Hence, the term "blood money." . . . To dream you are vomiting or otherwise shedding impure blood presages that you will be afflicted by a contagious disease, which you will pass on to others. Good blood flowing from a cut heralds psychosomatic illness.

BOMB—Back in the days when wars were romantic, *Napoleon's Book of Fate* could say without fear of contradiction: "If a fair maiden should dream of seeing a bombshell, she must look out for a brave artilleryman coming to ask her to be his bride. If she dreams she sees one of these articles explode, she will have great peace and comfort in her married life, a fond and faithful husband, and a happy family of handsome, dutiful sons and blooming daughters." Those days, however, vanished not long ago in a mushroom cloud. Today, any bomb symbolizes turmoil and trouble, out of which may come understanding—perhaps in the nick of time; perhaps too late.

BULL—If you dream that you are fleeing an enraged bull, your enemies will stop at nothing to destroy you and those you hold dear. Rest easy, however, for they will ultimately fail. If the bull should gore you in your dream, someone in a very high position is out to get you. He may succeed. You would be surprised that anyone so high up has even taken notice of you. If it is any consolation, you will drag him down with you—and he has very far to fall.

BURGLARS—See GHOSTS.

BUTCHERS—"To dream of butchers, who knock down, kill, cut, and divide beasts and afterwards sell them signifies danger and hurt and death to the sick, for it is their trade to divide and sell that which is dead," one dream manual begins a trifle antagonistically. In all fairness to your neighborhood butcher, you should not be frightened out of your wits when he appears in your dream. Your dream may portend nothing worse than short-weighting at the supermarket. . . . To vegetarians, in fact, visions of butchers are excellent Dreams of Convenience. If a vegetarian dreams of butchers and eats meat in his sleep, he will find it easier to remain steadfast to his vows during the waking day.

C

CAGE—If a maiden dreams that she frees a bird from a cage, her chastity is in danger. If a young man has the same dream, he may lose his inhibitions and threaten the chastity of his entire community. If a dreamer sees birds or animals in cages and does nothing to liberate them, the dreamer's business will prosper provided that he minds it.

CANDLE—A phallic dream, as are dreams of nail files, sticks, tree trunks, umbrellas, neckties, swords, plowshares, hammers, guns, peaks, airplanes, rockets, bananas, triangles, spears, torches, flagpoles, giraffes, tripods, girders, the Washington Monument, pencils, and phalli—according to recent Freudian interpretations. For a complete list, see your psychiatrist. . . . Whether or not you keep all this in mind, a dream of a candle that is extinguished signifies impotence. A candle burning at both ends: renewed vigor with a threat of infidelity. A candle burning brightly in the customary fashion: recovery and health. To dream of unlighted candles predicts that you will be rewarded undeservedly. To dream of candles flickering uneasily indicates that your sweetheart may or may not recover from a severe attack of melancholia. To dream that you make candlesticks in the company of butchers and bakers is a regression to childhood.

CARVING—In general, carving meat or fowl in a dream is a good omen denoting prosperity, comfort, and a future as a philanthropist. It sometimes implies enemies, but they will fail. In a few isolated cases, it has hinted at homicidal mania. . . . Havelock Ellis has written, almost gloatingly, about a lady who carved a duck at dinner and, later that night, dreamed of guillotining her husband. I once had a prophetic dream that was almost the reverse.

CATS—All cats are gray in the night, particularly in dreams. Any cat dream indicates some degree of treachery, particularly when you dream of a tame cat. This means someone you trust implicitly will betray you. It may be your servant; it may be your lover; it may be your spouse. Be careful. Trust nobody. To dream that you kill a cat means that you will discover treachery very soon. One dream manual intones: "To dream of one black cat is an indication that there is a neglected grave, and that it is your duty and privilege to go and tend it."

CHASE—See PURSUIT.

CHEEKS—To dream that one's cheeks are plump is good; if they are pink, so much the better. To dream that one's cheeks are purple has two meanings: there is a tinge of decadence about the dreamer . . . and he dreams in color.

CHERRIES—Among people who know dreams best, cherries are bad. "To dream of cherries indicates disappointment in life, vexation in the married state, and slight in love," says Anna Eva Fay. "To dream that you are picking cherries out of season portends that you will suffer some annoyance," says Leo Francis in *Dreams and their Meaning*. To dream, however, that you are picking or eating cherries in season means that you will seek illicit pleasures and perhaps you will indulge in them without being penalized. Perhaps not. . . . It is never good—in dreams or elsewhere—to engage in conversation with a stranger whose mouth is stuffed with cherries.

CITY—"I dreamed of a vast city—one that was not of God, but built by the hands of Evil," said Klopstock, a fifteenth-century German dream interpreter. Five centuries later, his disciples—known as Klopstockians or Klopstockings—still perpetuate his pessimistic theory. One of them has written: "This is a prophetic dream of the next state of the world, which we are rapidly approaching. . . . The peoples of the world are growing more and more slave-minded. . . . There will be, for the space of seven centuries, a world in chains." Awaken!

CLOCK—In modern context, a dream that a clock falls or breaks is an omen that radioactive fallout—of an unspecified dosage—is near. (This dream used to imply nothing more ominous than the approach of bubonic plague.) Fortunately, very few clocks have accidents in dreams. . . . As for clocks that don't fall, but just strike, they portend hasty marriage and some affluence, but of an uncertain degree. ("You will be *very* comfortable," says one dream book. *"Moderately,"* says another.)

Try to note what hour the clock strikes in your dream. All interpreters agree that if it strikes any hour before noon, it is better than if it strikes a P.M. hour. . . . If the clock is not ticking, you are likely to be unpunctual—if you are not already. If its alarm goes off, perhaps it is time for you to get up. . . . If a sick person dreams that a clock is ticking and then it stops, his time is truly running out.

CLOVER—To see yourself frolicking in a field composed entirely of four-leaf clovers indicates that you will make several happy marriages. . . . To see just one four-leaf clover indicates that you will make only one happy marriage, but this, too, is excellent. . . . Should you dream of other types of clover, you will be virtuous to a fault. Try to unbend a little.

COAL—A dark dream indeed! If you see coals extinguished, someone will surely die—if not you, then a close relative or friend. If you are spared death, the reprieve will prove temporary. In the meantime, do not be unprepared for penury. . . . If the coals still burn—however faintly—then you may anticipate nothing worse than shame, reproach, and perhaps a minor disappointment in love. . . . Dreaming of coal mines is better, provided you see no coal. *Old Aunt Dinah's Sure Guide to Lucky Dreams* offers this special insight into coal-mining dreams: "To dream of being in the bottom of coal-pits signifies marrying with a widow, for he that marries her shall never sound the depth of her. . . ." Old Aunt Dinah then quotes a client named Weller who told his son in atrocious dialect: "One vidder, Samivel, is more cunning than, I b'leeve they say, five-and-twenty common wimmen, and I won't be right certain if it ain't thirty." It is not known whether Old Aunt Dinah herself is a widow woman, but nothing about her would surprise me.

CODPIECE—Adjust your clothing before leaving.

COOK—"Dream you're busy with a cook
And for a wedding shortly look."
—Anna Eva Fay

This dream interpretation is confirmed by an unsolicited letter from a soldier stationed on Okinawa. He wrote me that he dreamed he was marrying his mess sergeant. Since this violated every military and social taboo on Okinawa, I dismissed it as foolishness. It was and it wasn't. I asked the G.I. to keep me posted on subsequent happenings and, four months later, I received a wedding announcement: The soldier had just married the daughter of a socially prominent native family. Two months thereafter, he became a father. Clearly, the age of miracles still persists on Okinawa as well as in dreams.

CORSET—See GIRDLE.

CROCODILE—"If a man sees himself in a dream eating crocodile flesh, he will rule as an official among his own people," says a 4,000-year-old Egyptian document intriguingly called "The Chester Beatty Papyrus." (How it got this name is a story in itself. To the best of my knowledge, there never was an Egyptian named Chester Beatty. Many centuries after it was written, however, the Englishman who donated this valuable papyrus to the British Museum happened to be named Chester Beatty.) Even today, the Chester Beatty Papyrus interpretation persists: Many a gimlet-eyed politician has risen to power soon after dreaming of eating crocodile flesh. . . . If a person with no political ambitions dreams of crocodiles, he is likely to be robbed. If planning a sea voyage, beware of pirates. A general admonition about crocodiles from *The Universal Dreamer*: "After such a dream, conduct yourself cautiously, for it will require all your skill to prevent being totally ruined and ending your days in a prison."

CUCUMBERS—"I like cucumbers, but cucumbers don't like me," a jovial but visibly uncomfortable dream interpreter once remarked astutely. It is never good to *befriend* a cucumber in your dream. To dream of *eating* cucumbers portends frustration to all but the sick, who will recover.

D

DAIRY—To dream that you are in a dairy churning butter, candling eggs, skimming milk, or indulging in other bucolic folkways means that you will marry a homespun person, have many children, and live a placid, contented life. If, however, a farmer's daughter or a dairymaid dreams of this, she is weak in worldy wisdom and may succumb to the wiles of the first traveling salesman who comes her way. If she does, he will love her and leave her. Worst of all, he will tell smutty stories about her in smoking cars.

DAISY—It is good for people to dream of daisies in spring or summer; it is a bad dream in fall or winter.

THE DEAD—To dream of seeing a dead friend or relative means that a living friend or relative will die. If the deceased appears contented in your dream, someone still will die—but your own health will prosper and you will glow like wax fruit. If you dream that you are speaking to the dead, you will have news within seventy-two hours. If you have physical contact with the dead person in your dream, the news will be evil indeed.

DEATH—"To dream you see this grim-looking bundle of bones," Miss Anna Eva Fay confided many years ago, "denotes that you will either be speedily married yourself or else assist at a wedding. To dream that you are dead denotes a speedy marriage." Anna Eva Fay's erstwhile contemporary, Dr. Sigmund Freud, took an entirely different tack. Dreams of the death of loved ones were, he said, simply Freudian wish-fulfillment. Mind you, said Freud, if you dream that your father, mother, sister, and brother are dead, this doesn't mean that you wish them dead *now*. But once upon a time, you did. Probably that wish crossed your mind in childhood; to a child, being dead means no more than being away. . . . In general, a boy dreams of his father's death while a girl dreams of her mother's death. If you accept the theory that every boy sees Dad as a rival for Mom's love (as well as the theory's feminine corollary), you can see what Freud was getting at—*incest!* And it gets worse as time goes by. According to Freud: "The daughter grows up and finds herself watched by the mother when she longs for real sexual freedom, while the mother is reminded by the budding beauty of her daughter that for her the time has come to renounce sexual claims." Dreams in which a child wishes his parents dead can often do great harm if repressed. Freud knew of a young man who, at seven, wished to push his father off a mountain top. *This was perfectly normal!* But at thirty, the young man was locking himself in his room because he feared that if he roamed the streets of Vienna, he would kill total strangers. *This was sick!*

DICE—To dream of crap-shooting is a sign of stability and imminent good fortune. By gratifying your impulse to gamble in your dreams, you can maintain your impressive air of fiscal responsibility during waking hours.

DIVORCE—This is a dream of contrary. If a married person dreams of suing for divorce, the fidelity of his or her mate is certain. You have no ground for jealousy. . . . If you should dream of divorce and then have trouble with your mate in waking life, see a marriage counselor —not a dream analyst.

DOCTOR—Dreams about doctors hold infinite promise. If a doctor is treating you, soon you will make a favorable impression on those whose esteem you value. If you dream that a doctor of the opposite sex is making love to you, then you will soon become enamored of a doctor, a medical student, or a veterinarian with an irresistible bedside manner. . . . If you are a mother and you dream of feeding a doctor, your oldest boy will enroll in medical school.

DOGS—Let sleeping dogs lie. If sleeping people dream of dogs, they should make careful note of the dogs' behavior. If a dog barks in your dream, beware of fiscal quarrels. If man's best friend bites you, beware of your human best friends. If you conquer a mad dog, many obstacles will be removed from your life—but beware of rabies! If a dog drools or fawns all over you, life will go well with you. If a dog gives birth to puppies, an apparent disappointment will work out in your favor. If a surly mutt snarls at you, be careful of your sweetheart—which is sound advice even should you never dream of dogs.

DOLPHIN—Many good things have been said of dolphins lately, but to dream of a dolphin portends a shattered romance. If the dolphin is out of water, it signifies the death of a friend. In general, dreams of dolphins denote insecurity. You have probably read too much propaganda recently about dolphins being smarter than people. It is enough to make any man fear that, even if he should survive automation, he will be replaced on his job by some sleek-looking porpoise. This is unlikely.

DONKEY—See ASS.

DOUGHNUT—If you dream of doughnuts, you will either get rich or go mad. The optimistic school of dream interpretation sees the doughnut; the pessimistic school sees the hole. The Freudians see sex.

DROWN—A dream of someone else's drowning foreshadows good business for the dreamer—especially if he be a lifeguard. If you are in love, your sweetheart is affable and marriage-minded. To dream that you see yourself drowning is a bad omen. It is always better to see someone else drowning. For one thing, you sleep better.

DWARFS—Dreaming about dwarfs didn't do Snow White or Walt Disney any harm. What's good for Walt Disney can be good for you, too. If you dream you see a dwarf, you will be promoted—out of kindergarten . . . out of the ranks . . . out of the steno pool, etc. You can write your own ticket.

E

EAT—Eating great gobs of food in a dream depicts a cannibalistic urge to eliminate one's rivals—particularly brothers and sisters competing for parental affection— by devouring them. There is nothing particularly distressing about this urge, according to Freud and others who should know. . . . The famous case of Oedipus Rex —who was deprived by circumstances of this dream— is a classic example of the food dream's importance to man. Because of his inability to dream of food, Oedipus grew up to kill his father, marry his mother, and put out his own eyes. Sophocles—playwright, poet, and amateur detective extraordinary—has described Oedipus' behavior far better than the most detailed psychiatric case history. And he did so without once mentioning an Oedipus Complex! Sophocles once remarked that:

> . . . many a man hath seen himself in dreams
> His mother's mate, but he who gives no heed
> To suchlike matters bears the easier life.

In waking life, Oedipus compensated for the dream activity he had been missing out on. There is much food for thought in dreams of eating.

EEL—It is never good to dream of eels, but if you see one in your dream, hang on to it. If it does not elude you, you will retain all you have, although you may never acquire more. If it wriggles from your grasp, your downfall is inevitable. . . . If you dream of buying or selling eels, you will engage in transactions with slippery partners.

EGGS—To dream of eggs is to keep your sunny side up, up. . . . Egg dreams are so wholesome that they can even offset most of the calamities promised by dreams of bacon. Thus, to dream of bacon-and-eggs means little or no harm will befall you. Dreams of eggs without bacon once drove an otherwise dignified dream interpreter to chant boisterously:

> To dream of eggs will profit give
> And show that thou shalt thrive and live.

It is good to know that dream interpreters champion eggs so ardently, for eggs have taken a bad beating lately in this cholesterol-conscious country of ours. Here are just a few of the many kind words about the eggs of your dreams: "To dream of seeing a great number of eggs indicates success in trade and in love. It also denotes a happy marriage and good children and great prosperity." . . . "To dream of eggs means that money is coming to you. If you dream that you find a nest of eggs, you will have a successful and happy life." . . ."To dream you are buying or selling eggs is a very favorable omen; whatever you are about will succeed, whether it be in love, trade, or finding a home." . . . "To dream that you are eating eggs denotes that you will shortly have a child and your affairs will go well." . . . "To dream of eggs signifies gain and profit, especially to physicians and painters and those who sell and trade with them." . . . "The childless married woman or the recent bride may expect to conceive after the dream of the egg. This vision brings a new hope of fulfillment to the wife of ten years or more in whose marriage bed there has never been a suckling. But if the woman knows herself to be physically quite incapable of childbirth, then it recommends adoption. The societies have long waiting lists of little mites to whom it is some childless couple's duty to bring the joy of a fragrant life. There will be no less happiness for the adoptive parents."

ELOPEMENT—You are headed down the ladder. If you are already married and have such a bigamous dream, you are unworthy of the position you occupy— at home, at work, and particularly at play. If you are unmarried and dream of elopement, you will have an unhappy marriage. If you are engaged, think twice. . . . If you dream that your betrothed has eloped with another, abandon hope: The odds are great indeed that you have already been betrayed.

EXAMS—Like many well-adjusted people, Sigmund Freud dreamed regularly that he was back in school taking an examination, which he often failed or had to repeat. This is a routine anxiety dream. One scientist noted that examination dreams occur only to persons who have passed exams, never to those who have flunked. Freud confirmed this with typical candor: "I failed in my examination for the doctor's degree in medical jurisprudence; never once has the matter worried me in my dreams. . . . In my dreams of school examinations I am always examined in history, a subject in which I passed brilliantly. . . ." Sometimes, examination dreams have tragic aftermaths—particularly among schoolboys. A few times each year, we read of students who, after recurrent dreams of failure, have committed suicide. As Professor Dirk Van Huyt lamented in one such case: "This dream is invariably a liar, and seems to have been thrust into the boy's subconscious by some malicious, lethally-minded imp from the Outer Spaces. The records tell us that it is never the dull lad who has this dream, which is a product of overanxiety from which dullness does not suffer much. It is always the brightest boy of his year, one of whom the head teacher says, "He was simply bound to pass." If your son is a brilliant worrier who suffers from examination dreams, it is not wise to send him to boarding school.

F

FAIRY—"A very favorable dream," says *Everybody's Dream Book*, which ought to know. "Beggars have had this dream and afterwards become very rich. Happy man! A noble wife for thee and a rich dowry, too. Happy woman! Thou wilt find a husband indeed. The laboring man, the trader, who dreams this dream shall rapidly rise into independence." Anna Eva Fay, however, gives fairy dreams a split decision: "For a maiden to dream she sees a fairy shows she will soon change her present state by becoming the wife of a good husband. It is good for women under any circumstances to dream of fairies; but it denotes evil to men and no man should undertake any important matter for several days after or it will surely end in his being disappointed." Shakespeare, in *Romeo and Juliet*, attributed dreams to Queen Mab, "the fairies' midwife," who, he claimed:

> . . . gallops night by night
> Through lovers' brains, and then they dream of love: . . . .
>
> O'er lawyers' fingers, who straight dream on fees;
> O'er ladies' lips, who straight on kisses dream: . . . .
>
> Sometimes she driveth o'er a soldier's neck,
> And then he dreams of cutting foreign throats. . . .

An earthier approach to fairies, dreams, and Shakespeare was taken by Dorothy L. Sayers, the twentieth century mystery writer:

> I am better off with vegetables
> At the bottom of my garden
> Than with all the fairies of the Midsummer Night's Dream.

FALLING—"It has many times happened to me to dream that I was falling down from a tower and never coming to the ground and when I awoke from the dream to find myself as weak and shaken as if I had really fallen," said the innkeeper's daughter in *Don Quixote*, written more than three centuries ago by a perceptive Spaniard. . . . Throughout history, dreams of falling have ranked among the Top Ten most prevalent dreams. Havelock Ellis contended that they may often occur in epileptic fits or other circulatory and nervous disturbances during sleep. . . . Freud said falling dreams symbolized surrender to erotic temptation. . . . *Old Aunt Dinah's Sure Guide to Lucky Dreams* disagrees in depth with Freud. Says Old Aunt Dinah: "If a person dreams that he has had a fall from his seat and would fain rise again, but cannot, it denotes that such a one shall lose the favor of some person who shall in vain seek to regain it. But, if he dreams that he got into his seat again, it betokens that he shall be restored to favor as formerly. Falling from a high tower in your dream doth intimate either a dejection of your spirits or some loss or cross suddenly to happen." . . . Professor Dirk Van Huyt cautions: "If a girl dreams this, she should take precautions against becoming a " 'fallen woman.' "

FAT—To dream you are fat is atrocious. If you dream that you have grown so fat as to surround yourself, you will be offered a chance to move to better surroundings, but you will be unable to accept because you will already have yourself hemmed in by family obligations, debt, or sluggishness.

FATHER—To see your father in a dream is a good omen. If he speaks to you, pay heed to what he says. His advice will come in handy sooner than you think.

FIRE—A great astrologer, Benevant, once said: "Thou hast dreamed of fire, hast thou? Why, thou hast hath a luck dream. It doth betoken for thee health and great happiness, kind kinsmen, and warm comrades. And, if a young lady and gentleman should thus dream, then that which thou sigheth for, craveth, and weepeth for —marriage!—shall soon be yours. Be of patience a little! But, if thou dreameth that thou art burned with the fire, it portendeth calamity and speech impediments!" . . . Freud said less eloquently: "The interpretation of dreams of fire justifies a prohibition of the nursery, which forbids children to 'play with fire' so that they may not wet the bed at night."

FISH—To dream that schools of fish are swimming in clear water means that you will be invited to the White House. To dream of dead fish means bad news has already happened, for does not yesterday's newspaper wrap today's fish? But to dream that you are *eating* fish indicates success in Wall Street. If a fish eludes your grasp, beware of slippery associates. . . . There are those who take a more clinical view of fish dreams. One of them was Dr. Marie de Manacéine, who noted: "Many people, when threatened by a gastric or intestinal attack, dream of seeing fish. The late Professor Sergius Botkine told me that he had found this coincidence in his own case, and I have myself several times found it in the case of a young girl who is well known to me. Some have supposed that the sleeping consciousness receives an impression of the elongated shape of the stomach or intestine, but such a supposition is easier to make than prove."

FLYING—Dreams of flying are even more common than dreams of falling—and they are common indeed! If you dream you are soaring all by yourself at great heights, you will soon achieve orgasm with one you love. Flying alone at a lower altitude is less promising, but still good. To fly between buildings and through streets, however, promises trouble and treason. Flying in an airplane means you will receive money. . . . In all fairness, I must point out that there are dissenters to these prevailing interpretations. *Napoleon's Oraculum* says chidingly: "For anyone to dream of flying implies that they are aspiring to something they will never be able to attain and unless speedily abandoned will end in their discomfiture and ruin." . . . Professor Dirk Van Huyt takes a literal view: "The single girl who has this dream may become an air hostess." . . . Says Freud: "The wish to be able to fly signifies in dreaming nothing else but the desire to be capable of sexual activities."

. . . While glancing over the January, 1879, issue of the *American Journal of Psychology,* I came across a theory of Professor Stanley Hall's. He said that dreams of flying date back to the good old evolutionary days when we all had gill slits. We didn't use our feet to navigate on water, he explained.

FLYING SAUCERS—See SAUCERS.

FOOD—See EAT.

FOX—If you dream of fighting a fox, you will become embroiled with a wily adversary. If you dream that you keep a tame fox as a house pet, you will love a bad-tempered shrew. If you marry her in the hope of taming such a shrew, you will be disappointed and perhaps cuckolded. Your divorce lawyer may even connive with her; his treachery will cost you heavily.

FROGS—All frog dreams are top-drawer.

G

GARLIC—See ONION.

GARTER—This is a dream foretelling an interlude of tawdry passion, perhaps with a chorus member. As the great Bavarian dream interpreter, Professor Ünrath, remarked in pre-Hitler days: "The romance may not be of storybook quality, but it will be none the less ideal. A love affair without wedding bells does not have to be devoid of harmony, say I."

GEESE—See GOOSE.

GENOCIDE—To dream that you exterminate a whole people is said to indicate that you are decisive, bold, courageous, and untroubled by conscience. You are likely to prove useful to society. "This may be so," one dream analyst remarked recently "but I'm damned if I'd want to entertain you in *my* home."

GHOST—If a ghost talks to you, you will come under some bad influence. The classic example is Hamlet, whose hobnobbing with his father's ghost led to his own early ghosthood. The case of Hamlet and his family has occasioned much hysteria and even outbursts of poetry, but it was treated very sanely for once in a recent, very Freudian film version called *The Rest is Silence*. The film was made in Germany, which remains a hotbed of Freudian thinking. It starred Hardy Kruger as Hamlet, whom the moviemakers had re-named John Q. Claudius, a foreign student at Harvard. The ghost of his father calls him by phone. When John Q. Claudius hangs up, he asks the Harvard switchboard to trace the call. He is told that there was no call. It was all a dream or hallucination. This, at least, puts l'*affaire Hamlet* into some perspective. . . . Freud, who often seemed preoccupied with bed-wetting, said that dreams of ghosts, burglars, and robbers are designed to awaken children so they may visit the bathroom before anything embarrassing happens. Perhaps this puts Hamlet into even greater perspective.

GIANTS—Dreams of giants are good, but dreams of dwarfs are even better.

GIRDLE—"To dream that you are girt with an old girdle," Anna Eva Fay observed quaintly, "signifies labor and pains. A new girdle signifies honor."

GOD—To dream of God is encouraging—particularly if you are dying.

GOLD—This is indeed a dream of avarice. If you dream that you lose or spend gold, you will lose or spend your money. If you dream that you strike gold, you will become a miser. If you dream that you wear gold, you will be praised to your face and ridiculed behind your back.

If you dream of the gold vaults at Fort Knox, you will be drafted or you will marry a corporal.

GONDOLA—Dreaming of this charming but outmoded means of transport is as sexual as a Venetian *signorina* leaning out of her window in a Freudian slip. . . . If a man dreams of a gondola, he will prosper from conquests in the boudoir rather than at the conference table. If a woman dreams of a gondola, she will always have a bright future as a courtesan. If a child dreams of a gondola, he or she has set sail toward puberty and nothing can change the course.

GOOSE—Another controversial dream. "This is a bad one for a single man," says one no-nonsense dream book. "The woman he loves will prove a very silly, incompetent wife. She will be a regular gossip, never at peace with her neighbors and always quarreling with her husband. He had better surrender her to someone else." . . . But another book insists: "To dream of a goose is the forerunner of good; expect soon to see a long absent friend. Geese denote success and riches to the dreamer in the furtherance of his pursuits. In love, they augur speedy marriage and fidelity in your sweetheart." . . . Since it is not wise to straddle the goose question, I take the pessimistic view, although I stop short of telling the dreamer to surrender his wife.

GOSPEL—See HYMN.

GREASE—See OIL.

GROWTHS—See WARTS.

H

HAIR—If you are a man and you dream that you have long, flowing locks, you have had a dream of effeminacy. You will prove cowardly and unmanly . . . "If a woman dreams that she has magnificent tresses, a million million golden tendrils," says a poetic dream interpreter of some repute, "then it means for her an abundance of love, which she should welcome without fear or inhibition. She will be caressed and pampered." If she dreams she is bald, she is prone to famine, poverty, or social diseases. But, if she dreams that she is wooed by a shiny-domed man, she will prosper. . . . If a hairy man dreams that he is bald, danger is lurking. If a bald man dreams that he is bald, he has little cause for alarm. . . . If any person dreams that his or her hair is kinky or knotted, the dreamer will reason illogically. . . . If a man sees his hair falling to the floor in a dream, he will lose money (someone may be misusing his charge account) or he will lose his job. Men contemplating a change of jobs often have this dream, for men who are rapidly losing their hair seem to be poor employment risks. Women who have the same dream are expressing fear that their sex appeal is waning.

HAIRCUT—Castration looms—at the hands of a member of the opposite sex.

HAM—See BACON.

HANDS—If you dream of possessing "the hands you love to touch," you are destined for an important assignment that will culminate in success. . . . If you dream of dishpan hands, you are likely to find yourself between frying pan and fire. . . . If a right-handed person dreams that he is left-handed, or vice versa, beware! . . . If you shake hands in a dream, Lady Luck will caress you. If your hands are tied, your hopes will be stymied. A burnt or withered hand signifies affliction.

HARVEST—To dream that you are harvesting any crop means that you will become a celebrity—perhaps even a darling of café society whose every utterance will be quoted and misquoted in the press. Try to remember that you will be setting an example for thousands of youngsters who will read avidly of your career. In any event, dreams of harvest contain a wealth of promise. For rustic dreamers, one interpreter writes: "The yellow, mellowed harvest, with its busy, merry workers, with the rolled sleeves of the men and their open, hairy chests: with the painted garments of the women, full-bosomed and happy with their burdens. . . . All this is pictorial of fulfillment of toil rewarded with Nature's bounty." He concludes with this admonition: "Spend the harvest of joy wisely, remembering that you must save the seed corn."

HEAD, LOSS OF—See AMPUTATION.

HILL—If you dream that you climb several hills, you will attain recognition—if not in your lifetime, then shortly after. As a philanthropist, you will do well to subsidize literary geniuses, who will compose poems and novels eulogizing you. But do not be taken in by beatniks. No matter what happens, your life insurance will grant you a smattering of immortality. . . . To dream that you are going downhill merely hints that you are going downhill.

HORN—If a man dreams that he has horns on his head, he should feel free to anticipate wealth, power, and perhaps a Cabinet post. But he should also take a few minutes to look into his wife's conduct.

HORNET—See BEE.

HORSE—If you dream that you are mounted upon a stately white horse which is your own, you will live with a gorgeous and generous wife. If the horse is not your own, you will live with someone else's gorgeous but generous wife. If you dream of riding a tired horse, you will be desperately in love with an older person who will nag you in your later years. If you see a dead horse, your business will deteriorate hopelessly—for, proverb-

ially speaking, "you can't get milk from a dead horse."
Black horses symbolize Death.

HOUSE—A vacant house denotes a barren woman.
Building a house means you will have a good marriage
that may yet be graced with progeny. . . . If you see a
house on fire, you will receive news that is hot off the
press. If it is your house that burns, the news will be sad
for you.

HUSBAND—If a woman dreams she is with her husband, she possesses a healthy respect for him. If she
dreams she is married to a man who is not her husband,
she must choose her words carefully in the other man's
presence.

HYMN—If you hear hymns, psalms, or even syncopated
gospel songs in your dream, your business will be hindered—perhaps deservedly. I know of a luncheonette
owner who was a pillar of his Southern community as
well as a dabbler in dream interpretation. One night, he
dreamed that a jukebox played a hymn called "Jesus
Was a White Man." Naturally, he was alarmed. The
next morning, however, the dream appeared to be refuted. If anything, business seemed to be picking up
rapidly at his luncheonette. By noon, it was packed—
by Negroes staging a sit-in and singing "We Shall Overcome."

I

ICE—Dreams of ice are dismal for city dwellers and
commuters. At the very least, a monumental traffic jam
will develop. . . . In rural America—where thirty per
cent of the population dwells—dreams of ice are always
good. Florida orange growers who dream of ice need not
shudder; theirs will be a good crop. The non-citrus
farmer can rejoice, too. He will be paid for growing

crops and he will be paid for not growing crops. Truly, the farmer is a blessed American.

IDIOT—"If anyone dreams that he is turned idiot or mad and is guilty of public extravagancies, he shall be long-lived, a favorite, and gain pleasure and profit by the people," said Anna Eva Fay. It is the way of the world that the idiots invariably succeed. . . . If you dream that you are a normal person who is approached by an idiot, buck up! This is a dream of contrary. It means you will marry someone intelligent who may not be much on looks.

ILLNESS—Are your vaccinations up to date? Smallpox can be a nasty business.

IVORY—A French dream interpreter in Poitiers reported to a learned journal that an elderly woman in rags approached him and offered her "life savings" if he would interpret her dream. Touched by her plea, he allowed the ragged lady the ten per cent discount given only to members of his immediate family. "I dreamed that I wore an ivory crown," the beggar woman told him. The dream interpreter shook her withered hand and congratulated her. "Old crone, this is a superior dream," he told her happily. "The dream of ivory prophesizes a smooth, unsullied romance. Especially to the young *ingenue* does it promise her a tall and lithe lover, whose prowess at *amour* is as magnificent as his sideburns." The old lady said: "That is all very well, but I am hardly a young *ingenue*." The gallant dream interpreter tried to tell her otherwise, but then capitulated. "In such a case," he said, "the dream of ivory portends beauty, sweetness, virtue, rare pleasures, and, above all, money! When the dream comes true, I trust you will repay the ten per cent discount I allowed you." . . . A week later, his prophecy gave every indication of having come true. He saw the old woman—clad in Balenciaga finery—cruising the streets of Poitiers in a chauffeur-driven Simca Aronde. To his disappointment, however, she avoided him. She never offered to pay up the ten per cent discount. When the dream interpreter sought her out, her butler told him rather haughtily: "She is in today, but she is always out to you." Eventually, the dream interpreter submitted his complaint to a board of impartial investigators. They learned that the lady had been wealthy all her life—"to the manor born," as the French say. With the astuteness that is granted only to the very rich, she had donned rags upon hearing that the local dream interpreter charged whatever the market would bear. The dispute is now awaiting arbitration.

JET PLANE—See FLYING.

JEWELS—Diamonds are a dreamer's best friend, although even the cheapest bauble is a pleasant trifle. Any jewelry dream is fortuitous. If your lover bedecks you with jewels, his object is matrimony. If he pawns your jewels, his object is parsimony—which can be a virtue, too. . . . If you see your lover bedecked in jewels, you will marry in haste, but never repent. . . . If you are counting jewels, you will have many children and they will all be healthy. If you find jewels, your sexual powers will flourish, but do not squander them.

JUMP—To dream that you jump over bridges portends that you will have to see your dentist soon, but, through courage, fortitude, and teamwork, the two of you will overcome the ravages of tooth decay. In general, jumping is an optimistic dream telling that obstacles will be overcome.

JURY—If you dream that a jury is trying you, your sweetheart or mate will abandon you, but you will take a long voyage and find a better partner for yourself. If you dream that the jury acquits you, your new partner and you will have exciting, romantic adventures ending in the death of one of you. If the dream jury condemns you, then you and your new partner will live happily ever after. Throughout history, juries have done some mighty strange things, but dreams have been even more perverse.

JUSTICE OF THE PEACE—To envision one of these genial, worthy gentlemen is a disturbing dream of contrary: Your marriage may be illegal. Check all your documents for legal loopholes.

K

KEY—"To dream your keys are gone or lost
    Denotes that you'll be vexed or crossed."
                    —Anna Eva Fay

Freud would have gone along with this interpretation, but he would certainly have been more explicit. He would have seen it as a dream of castration or impotence. To him, the familiar combination of lock and key symbolized sexual intercourse. . . . If you dream of finding a key, you will have a child. If you see yourself giving your key to another, you will marry soon. If you dream of a skeleton key, you will marry an emaciated person out of pity, which may one day grow into true love.

KILL—If you see anyone killing a bird or beast in your dream, your loved one is on the verge of deserting you. To a married woman, such a dream may also mean that a false friend of your husband's will make improper advances to you. Therefore, be on your guard with your husband's false friends. . . . If you dream that you are killing a man or woman, you will be successful in some enterprise.

KISS—If a man dreams of attempting to kiss a very young girl who vanishes before he can fulfill his passion, he will be successful in love the next day. A portly businessman—who had given up chasing his agile and nubile young secretary around his desk several times a day—resumed his pursuit after this dream. Startled by this surprise attack, the secretary capitulated. . . . Dream researchers are currently delving rather deeply into dream kissing. Here are the preliminary findings of a team from a midwestern university: "Dream kissing is virtually asexual and seldom associated with any physical release. . . . Senior citizens often dream that childhood sweethearts are embracing them." These findings, it must be emphasized, are not yet final.

KNIFE—If you have any case pending in court and you dream of knives, plead guilty. Pay all parking tickets. Confess your sins. Knife dreams go particularly hard on those already in trouble. . . . If the innocent dream of knives, they will quarrel with friends, be assaulted on brightly lit streets, learn of marital infidelity, and undergo major surgery. . . . In general, anyone who dreams of knives will be accident prone; specifically, avoid such pastimes as mumblety-peg. Do not fraternize with competitors or ex-spouses.

L

LABOR—To dream that you do manual labor foreordains that your declining years will be spent in luxurious indolence. To dream that others labor indicates that your future lies in absentee ownership.

LADDER—The ancient Roman oracle, Sallustius Amicus, proclaimed this to be one of the most favorable of all dreams: "Lover, harken! Thou shalt kiss in wedlock thy coveted bride or thy longed-for bridegroom. Man of commerce, it bodes well for thee. Gentle zephyrs of fortune shall blow thee into harbors of independence. It portends wealth, honor, and godlike glory. Thou tiller of the soil, dost thou dream of climbing the ladder? Thy humus and thy manure shall bring forth amply and make thee rich. And thou, poor widow, if thou dreamest this dream, thou shalt light thy coal again and thy sorrow shall be turned into joy."

LAMB—Nobody can find fault with a dream of lambs. They symbolize comfort and prosperity. Even if they are being led to slaughter, they will prove palatable if cooked properly and served with mint jelly. . . . If a young woman dreams of lambs, her husband will be a practical joker, a live wire, the life of the party. She will stay home and bear him many fun-loving children. . . . If a young man dreams of frisking lambs, his wife will be young, beautiful and a virgin. She will also be naive and will tend to take his friends at face value. If there be ladykillers, seducers, or adulterers among his friends, he should keep her from them and them from her.

LAUGHTER—Dreams of laughter are always harbingers of approaching hysteria as well as the tragedy that induces it. Such dreams also denote loss of property and friends. Nobody should laugh in dreams. Nobody should laugh *at* dreams.

LEAP-FROG—If a man dreams that he is indulging in this popular American sport, troubles and complaints will overtake him by leaps and bounds. . . . If a woman has the same dream, her lover is inconstant, for he does not always have both feet on the ground. . . . If a child dreams of playing leap-frog, he should be given more outdoor recreation.

LEEKS—See ONION.

LETTUCE—If you eat lettuce in a dream, you will have difficulty managing your financial affairs. . . . It never pays to eat bacon, lettuce, and tomato sandwiches just before retiring. You may then dream of them. Dreams of bacon, as we have seen earlier, are all bad. The combination is frightening. A female who dreams of this tasty snack should never aspire to be treasurer of any women's organization.

LICE—"For a man to dream he is lousy and is much troubled with killing and destroying lice, it is a sign of getting much money and great riches."—*Old Aunt Dinah.*

LIGHTNING—In a dream, summer lightning unaccompanied by a storm indicates that you will be relocated. If lightning strikes directly in front of you, then your progress will be impeded. If your spouse is struck by lightning, your marriage bonds will be loosened. If you are struck by lightning in a dream, you need never fear lightning again—for it rarely strikes twice.

LIZARD—All dream interpreters but one have viewed the lizard as a warning of misery at the hands of secret enemies or unseen bacilli. If you experience this dream, do not eat lizard meat. If in Mexico, where lizards thrive, avoid lizards as well as unbottled water. . . . The noteworthy exception to this view was, as you may have guessed, Dr. Sigmund Freud. To him, the lizard was not merely a phallic symbol. It also represented castration insurance for it is, he noted, "an animal whose tail, if pulled off, is regenerated by a new growth."

LOBSTER—To dream of eating lobster portends a new love affair. If this tasty shellfish is highly seasoned, your new flame will be passionate, but generous with your money, affable to a fault, and not completely truthful. If it tastes bland, then your love affair will be matter-of-fact and stable, but hardly worth the trouble. If you see a lobster crawling in your dream, you will be humiliated. If it claws at you, expect a sudden visit from in-laws.

LOST—This is one of the most common of all dreams. In general, it is taken to imply self-punishment. The dreamer is depressed and feels an urgent need to be disciplined. It is a particularly recurrent dream among people who have committed perfect crimes. . . . Stammerers, Bohemians, sex deviates, and Southern Republicans have been known to dream that they are walking in the wrong direction. Some say that this dream epitomizes man's undying aspiration to make a living hell on earth. . . . If you dream of losing something or someone —be it your mother, yourself, or your most precious possession—it means that you really want to get rid of it. If you lose something and then find it again in a dream, it means that nothing is ever hopelessly lost.

LUCKY—This is a dream of contrary. To dream that you are lucky means most assuredly that you are out of luck.

M

MALT—See BEER.

MANURE—To dream that you shovel manure is not good for the city dweller, but it is excellent for rural Americans. To the city man, it indicates that he dislikes his job, but cannot afford to abandon it. To the city woman, it indicates insecurity about rearing her children in the asphalt jungle. To the city child, it portends that his parents or the Fresh Air Fund or some well-meaning benefactor will send the child to summer camp, where the child will suffer. But, to all country folk, dreams of manure symbolize fertile crops, good harvests, and bawdy stories well told.

MARMALADE—To dream that you are eating marmalade portends illness, vexation, harrassment, and bigotry. . . . To dream that you are making marmalade foreshadows a wedding at which you will be prominent. Shortly before my own wedding, I dreamed that I was making marmalade in a Pullman kitchen. Prophetic as the dream was, it proved even more significant when—among dozens of wedding gifts—my wife and I received no fewer than four marmalade servers. Since we seldom eat marmalade (and, when we do, we scoop it directly from a jar), we disposed of all four gifts with some difficulty. To this day, I classify all dreams of marmalade as true nightmares.

MARRIAGE—A dream of marriage implies certain death—a prophecy which, given time, has never proved false. Dreams of marriage also lead to bankruptcy courts, unemployment insurance lines, and prisons. Such dreams are particularly ominous for sailors, aviators, and astronauts; they should fully expect to be lost at sea, perhaps forever. . . . If, however, you dream that you are merely a best man, bridesmaid, usher, wine-taster, acolyte, flower girl, eunuch, or supporting performer at a wedding, you will be showered with blessings.

MARTYR—A dream of semi-contrary. If a man dreams that he dies for his religious or political beliefs, he will actually be slain or wounded by a jealous husband. No jury in the land will convict his assailant—and thus the dream prophecy will be fulfilled in an ironic way. . . . If a woman dreams that she is martyred, she has a distressing tendency toward narcissism and Joan-of-Arc complexes. . . . Martyr dreams are particularly prevalent among actresses and hypocrites.

MEASLES—You are about to become rich if you dream you have measles. Your fortune will come from an unexpected source—a long-lost relative, a forgotten investment, a rigged quiz show, or the like. But your riches will be accompanied by infamy. You will be shunned by respectable citizens, whom you will curse as you wend your profitable way from mansion to bank.

MICE—See MOUSE.

MILK—Anna Eva Fay saw it this way: "To drink your milk is an extraordinary good sign and to dream you see breasts of milk signifies profit. To dream you are carrying milk is a good sign, but, if you fall and spill it, misfortunes will befall you, from which it would be difficult to extricate yourself." This, as you might surmise, is a rather feminine view of milk dreams, but men don't often dream of milk. If a man should dream of milk, it would be wise for him to determine whether he was breast-fed or bottle-fed in early life. This should afford the first clue that may unravel his dream. . . .

MISSILES—Dreams of missiles have assumed the significance that dreams of swords used to possess. "He who dreams of the sword lives by the sword," a pre-Freudian dream interpreter once noted. Post-Freudian analysts have applied similar meanings to dreams of missiles. If a pacifist dreams of missiles, his is not a dream of contrary, but a revelation of his inner warlike nature—which may be why some pacifists are very militant people. . . . If you dream of missiles, walk softly and do not carry a big stick.

MOLES—See WARTS.

MONEY—Money is the stuff that too many dreams are made on. Money dreams occur even in cultures that have never heard of money. Some interpreters equate love with money, which is why divorcees and spinsters dream often of finding money while golddiggers dream of finding love. . . . Freud said that money represents a yearning for the uncleanliness of childhood. Some laymen contend that Freud found dirt everywhere. . . . A pioneer American dream interpreter wrote in 1795: "To dream of money signifies loss." But, nowadays, a man who dreams of losing money will be told that he is expressing fear of squandering his manhood. . . . In old people, dreams of losing money signify short life expectancies; in young people, prosperous times but short life expectancies. . . . Children who dream of money may be yearning for the uncleanliness of adult life. They should be watched carefully but discreetly by their parents.

MONSTER—All monsters are good.

MOUSE—To dream of mice is good for all dreamers, particularly cats. But cats are unskilled in even the rudiments of dream interpretation, which may be why cats have yet to inherit the earth despite the efforts of cat-lovers. . . . A rather Freudian interpretation of mice dreams reads: "Your subconscious is telling you to copy the virtues of mice: to be busy, observant, domestic, family-conscious, and fecund. You also hope that you will be as shiny-eyed and sleek as a gray mouse. But you also have a yearning to be diminished—to be reduced to mouselike proportions, to be small but dynamic, to travel through narrow passages, to be inconsequential. This, too, is good—if it's what you want."

MURDER—Many dream interpreters say that if you dream you commit murder, you are ashamed of how you make your money. I subscribe to this theory because I once studied the case of a young man whose father— a very suave, Continental type—made his fortune smuggling birth-control products into Mediterranean countries. The young man assumed a position with his father's business and excelled at it, but, when asked how he made a living, he would reply nonchalantly: "I'm in the export-import business." At night, however, he had a recurrent dream: He was beating his father to death with the hollowed cane that his dapper daddy used for smuggling purposes. Soon after his dream had been fully analyzed, the young man changed jobs and never again dreamed of murder. . . . Other dream interpreters take a more ritualistic view of murder. *Everybody's Dream Book* asserts: "It foretells your vicious life, the perpetration of evil, and possibly imprisonment. After such a dream, repent and abandon sin and evil associations or it will be dreadful for you." . . . Professor Dirk Van Huyt has an interesting theory about the dream of murder: "This may mean that you have been reading the gangster story or the thriller. . . . So far, it is harmless and you will not wake up emotionally exhausted. But if you find yourself in great tension, and seizing your sleeping spouse by the throat in your dream, better see a psychiatrist, and in the meantime take a sedative."

MUSIC—If you hear religious music, see the entry for *Hymns*. . . . If you hear symphonic music in your dream, your life will be long but complicated. Guard your hearing. . . . If you hear operatic music, beware of fat enchantresses. . . . If you hear show tunes, you will find your true love across a crowded room. . . . If you hear rock-'n'-roll, do not be surprised if you are

married in blue jeans at a midnight ceremony. But, if
yours is a mixed marriage, disaster will lurk. . . . If
you hear chamber music, bathe regularly and watch
personal hygiene at all times. . . . If the music is *a
cappella,* so to speak, you are doomed to be alone in life.

MUSTARD SEED—To dream that you see or eat this
barely recognizable growth is a bad omen for all. Epi-
demics loom.

N

NAILS—To dream that your nails are larger and pointier
than usual indicates that you will make money through
sharp practices; if the opposite, your blunt talk will cost
you customers. If you dream that your nails are removed
altogether, beware of castration by intimates. If you
dream that others' nails are pressing into your flesh, beware of crucifixion. If you dream of nail-biting, try to
curtail all nervous mannerisms: they are getting out of
control. For a man to see himself paring his own nails
several times in a single dream is a sure sign of latent
effeminacy.

NAKED—Certainly the most celebrated of all dreams.
If you've never experienced it, see your doctor and ask
him to make sure you're human. Those much-publicized
lovers—Adam and Eve—patrolled Paradise Gardens in
the raw. But today, society frowns on nudity even in
dreams, where Maidenform bras are often mandatory.
Those of us who dream repeatedly of running naked
through the streets would be classified as madmen by
many solid citizens and census takers in double-breasted
suits. Dreams still remain the last frontier of nudity. . . .
*A note for dreamers who are incurable prudes about
nudes:* If naked dreams truly offend you, the best way
to avoid them is to sleep in the raw. By gratifying your
repressed urge for nudity, you may stop dreaming about
it. . . . *Some more specific interpretations:* "To dream

...lat you are in a state of nudity foretells to a certainty poverty, disgrace, and misfortune." . . . "To persons in love it shows that they will never marry the present object of their affections. The person they will get instead will be cross-tempered, unkind, and self-indulgent." . . . "Nakedness symbolizes the exposure of the inner self to the judgment of others." . . . Naked man: fear and terror. . . . Naked woman: if she is young and fair, good luck; if an old crone, bad luck. . . . If you see your mate naked, you will excel in bed.

NAME—What's in a name? Any other dream would smell sweeter. If you dream that you have changed your name, you will never marry. If you dream that you are addressed by a wrong or improper name, you will be an innocent victim of mistaken identity.

NOSE, LOSS OF—See AMPUTATION.

O

OIL—To dream that you are anointed with oil, grease, suntan lotion, Man Tan or salad dressing indicates that you are on the way out. There is no choice but to go gracefully.

OLD MAN—If a woman dreams that she is courted by a dirty old man, she will one day marry for money. . . . If a man has the same dream, it has a subtle homosexual theme that he had best puzzle out for himself. . . . If a woman dreams that she is courted by a clean old man, her children will grow rich. . . . It is a particularly auspicious dream for aging spinsters.

OLD WOMAN—Professor Dirk Van Huyt waxes eloquent on the subject of old women in dreams: "Some elderly person has something to bestow on you. Not improbably it will be some work to do, but work which will prove a sheer delight instead of boredom, and it will be most handsomely rewarded. If the dreamer is a virgin, then the kindly old woman is come to promise her a prepossessing and physically fine lover, who will win her in marriage and give her bonny children. The virgin is promised the most rapturously satisfying of honeymoons and from the night of this dream she is no longer to be shy when wooed. All will come right."

ONIONS—Much bloode in they domestic scenes
　　　　Secrets tolde or else betrayed
　　　　And daintye falsehoods made and said."
　　　　"To dreame of eating onions means
　　　　　　　　　—from an ancient dream book

To dream nowadays that you are eating onions, garlic or leeks portends nothing worse than bad breath. . . . To dream of paring onions means that you'll cry tomorrow. . . . To dream that a sick friend gives you onions implies that your friend will get over a sickness by transmitting it to you. . . . If you dream of onions, hoard your courage.

ORGAN—To dream of organs and organ music signifies extreme joy. If you are seeking a more Freudian interpretation, look elsewhere.

ORPHANS—Anyone who dreams of orphans will receive bequests from strangers—perhaps money or perhaps an unidentified child left on the doorstep. . . . If a man dreams of an attractive orphan, he will marry a woman with great inherited wealth. . . . But even the ugliest orphan is well worth dreaming about. If you cannot adopt one, the next best way to induce such a dream is to take an orphan to lunch. . . . If your child dreams that he or she is an orphan, the child wishes that you and your spouse were dead. There is nothing particularly wrong with your child. Neither Dr. Freud nor Dr. Spock would view this dream with undue alarm, so why should you?

OVEN—To dream of an oven burning hot signifies change of address. To dream it burns cold signifies change of life.

OWL—To dream of this bird of night betokens melancholia. If you hear an owl hoot, gird yourself for sickness, poverty, and exposure. If you see a silent owl, you will lose naught, but your zest for the pleasures of life will diminish. . . . Grim as my view of the owl may be, it seems rosy when placed alongside that of a European dream interpreter: "There bodes no good for anybody in the dream of the owl. . . . The owl does not foretell any general threat, like war or famine, but appears in dream only to the person who is most in jeopardy. Be you man or woman, does some sex marauder threaten your love life? Is there a harpy with designs upon your man, or does some dishonest, dashing seducer have designs upon your sweetheart or your wife? It would be well to ascertain. Watch, but pray, too. Is somebody poisoning the mind of your employer with respect to your ability and conscientiousness? Are your children well out of the way of danger? Is it that you are living in conditions unwholesome for them? Get out of the habitation and the very district, no matter what it costs you. Are your savings deposited in a trustworthy place? If not, remove them to safer custody. Is somebody tempting you to an investment which could spell ruin? Are the minds of your friends being poisoned with respect to your sincerity and morals?" Disciples of this particular dream interpreter report that dreams of owls are invariably preludes to insomnia.

P

PALM—In dreams as in the Bible, the palm is a symbol of righteousness and he who is inspired by such a dream will flourish like a cedar in Lebanon. She who dreams of the palm will bear many children.

PANTOMIME—If there are no sounds in your dream, you are rebuking yourself for not having listened attentively to someone who was addressing you.

PARALYSIS—See APPOINTMENT.

PARROT—If you dream of many parrots chattering, you will be slandered unmercifully when you are away from home. What can you do to defeat these evil rumors? Rise above them. Or live them down. Or stay home. . . . If you dream of owning a single parrot, you will spend your life with an overly talkative mate. . . . To dream that you see many silent parrots predicts that you will leave the country, settle elsewhere, marry a native of your new land, live happily, cultivate soil, amass great wealth, and have two children—a boy who will devote his life to the church or public service and a girl who will marry a billionaire. In the end, you will die, but you may be remembered for a while.

PEACHES—If you dream of peaches when they are in season, you will earn the love and friendship of all. If peaches are out of season, it is a bad omen.

PEARLS—Do not cast them before swine. In dreams, pearls symbolize tears or sorrow. If a woman dreams that her neck is hung with pearls, she will come to grief because of her own loose talk. Every woman is her own *femme fatale*.

PHYSICIAN—See DOCTOR.

PIGEONS—To dream of pigeons is always good. If you see these adorable birds hovering over you, anticipate heavenly droppings. No matter what context you see pigeons in, you will have a happy home if you lead a clean life.

PLANE—See JET PLANE.

PLANT—To dream that any plants grow out of your body is a malignant dream foreshadowing your certain death. . . . To see plants growing in a normal manner is heartening, whether you see them in dreams or in flower pots.

POND—A dream of a small pond tells a man that a beautiful woman loves him, but fears to express her affection because it may be unrequited. If the man is available or interested, he should keep his ears open. Within a week, a woman will say something of apparent innocence (but with a subtle second meaning) to him—and then he will know. . . . If a woman dreams of a stagnant pond, it is prophetic of menopause; of two ponds, menopause and death.

POPE—If your dream involves the Pope or a Popish plot, you will soon visit Italy. But to priests, cardinals, bishops and other churchmen, such a dream has quite a different meaning.

PORK—See BACON.

PORPOISE—See DOLPHIN.

POT ROAST—See ROAST BEEF.

POVERTY—To dream of dwelling in poverty is nothing new to many of us, but it promises disaster for feather merchants, confidence men, wheeler-dealers, disc jockeys, and others who live by their wits. To most others, it merely indicates that they may be living above their incomes, but they are helping to keep the economy strong. To the happy few who are well fixed in life, it is merely another reminder that nothing lasts forever.

PRECIPICE—A dream of precipices foretells that your body or spirit will be maimed by one who truly wishes you well, but who is clumsy. Do not ride in friends' cars. Do not climb mountains. Precipices never bode well.

PREGNANT—If a pregnant woman dreams that she is pregnant, she will give birth to twins at the appropriate time. If a married woman dreams that she is pregnant, but she is definitely not, her husband is likely to succumb to misogyny. If an unmarried woman dreams that she is pregnant, she will be involved in a scandal. A marriage counselor adds: "A wavering virgin who has such a dream should not surrender her chastity until she is safely married. Her subconscious may be tricking her into abandoning virtue for passion. But dreams know nothing about our system of Western morals, which imposes a lifetime of hardship upon the child conceived out of wedlock." If a man dreams he is pregnant, he will make a disastrous marriage.

PSALM—See HYMN.

PURSUIT—Whether you are the pursued or the pursuer, such a dream is an aggressive dream, according to Freud. . . . Others say that dreams of pursuit denote fear of sexual injury. Guard your genitals.

PUSTULES—See WARTS.

Q

QUACKS—To dream that you are in the care of a quack is unfortunate, but not uncommon. Beware of these menaces to society, but maintain a forgiving disposition because most of them are good people—like you and me—who somehow have gone astray or perhaps were born with a missing connection. Many people like to switch dream interpreters after dreaming of quacks, but such are the hazards of this often maligned profession of ours.

QUICKSAND—To dream that you are wallowing in muck and mire implies that you dwell with many temptations and evil urges that you know nothing about. Guard yourself against your basest instincts. Avoid hasty decisions, loose morality, and unbridled passions. If you dream that someone is rescuing you from quicksand, your life will be salvaged by a good marriage. If you see another person sinking in quicksand, try to give him a hand.

R

RABBITS—If you dream that you see rabbits in profusion, you will soon change your address and begin a new life. You will marry and dwell in a large city whose population you will swell considerably. For senior citizens nowadays, rabbit dreams mean removal to St. Petersburg and unexpected parenthood in the twilight years. And for playboys, dreams of bunnies may merely imply membership in key clubs.

RACE—To dream you are running a race betokens good to all but sick people. Sick people should stay in bed and dream, not run races. . . . But, in almost all other cases, dreams of racing imply many rewarding erotic adventures ahead. Racing is always a fortuitous dream for harlots and horsemen.

RADISHES—To dream of radishes tells you that you have a cast-iron stomach. You can eat anything—and probably will for as long as you are among the living. But guard against ulcers.

RAINBOW—In ancient Greece, a dream of rainbows was good for men in trouble, but bad for contented men. Today it also means a change of status, success in foreign trade, travel in first-class accommodations, and elegantly furnished hotels of the highest caliber. . . . If the rainbow is in the eastern sky, the sick will get money and the poor will have their health. . . . If it is in the west, the rich will get richer and the poor will multiply.

RAVEN—This noble, upright bird once had a very favorable dream image. Early in the nineteenth century, however, the raven became associated with the dissolute and distinctly anti-social life of one Edgar Allan Poe.

By the end of the nineteenth century, even such un-biased dream interpreters as Anna Eva Fay could be labeled "anti-raven." Said Miss Fay: "To dream you see a raven is a very unfavorable token. It denotes mischief and adversity. In love, it shows falsehood. To the married, it forebodes much mischief. To the sailor it betokens shipwreck and much distress on a foreign shore."

RESCUE—Freud, whose discernment in such matters was unparalleled, associated dreams of rescue with re-production. He said: "To rescue, especially to rescue from the water, is, when dreamed by a woman, equiv-alent to giving birth; this sense is, however, modified when the dreamer is a man." I suspect Freud goes a trifle overboard when he calls such a dream the "equiv-alent" of giving birth. Many mothers, I am sure, will disagree with him.

RICE—To dream of rice portends that you will marry.

RIDING—To dream that one is traveling in a parlor car or other first-class accommodations when one is accustomed to humbler modes indicates that the dreamer will abuse expense accounts or allow vanity to lead to debt. Otherwise, all riding dreams are merely sexual.

RIVER—Crossing a river (which ranks among the dozen most common occurrences in dreams) often rep-resents a decisive step away from mental illness, an escape from parental domination, the emergence into puberty, or a summoning of courage. . . . If you dream that you go back and forth across a river by ferry, you are chiding yourself for indecisiveness. Bureaucrats have this dream frequently.

ROAST BEEF—This and all others of its ilk (dreams of sauerbraten, pot roast, rump roast, and even of delicatessen) are gluttonous dreams.

ROBBERS—See GHOSTS.

ROT—Shun venereal disease and its carriers. Lead an upright existence. Bathe before bedtime. Sleep with your window open. Ultimately, this dream will fade.

ROUSE—See AROUSE.

RUMP—See ROAST BEEF.

S

SAUCERS, FLYING—Depending on which school of thought you pay your dues to, a dream of flying saucers is either a dream of returning to the womb or a dream of God. I reject the womb theory because it is too vague. After all, more than half of any dream interpreter's clientele is trying to return to the womb by various Freudian means, of which flying saucers are just one modern variation. . . . I subscribe to the God theory because it is so much more concrete. The flying saucer is clearly the eye of God searching out all men's souls. But it is not considered sophisticated these days to dream of God and so we disguise it as a flying saucer dream. Thus, it becomes a respectable, pragmatic, and scientific dream—with a sly sense of humor.

SAUERBRATEN—See ROAST BEEF.

SAUSAGE—See BACON.

SCHOOL—If an adult dreams of beginning school again and not doing so well as might be expected, the dreamer is on the verge of getting in over his or her head in some undertaking. . . . If a child dreams of being in school, good! . . . A seventeenth-century Cambridge University mathematics teacher named Barrow is rumored to have had a dream that he was a pupil being taught by one of his students. Barrow met the dream halfway. He resigned on condition that the pupil be appointed in his place. The pupil's name was Sir Isaac Newton. . . . No matter what a teacher dreams, it is seldom necessary nowadays to take drastic measures like Barrow's.

SERPENT—See SNAKE.

SERVANT—To dream that you discharge a servant portends a domestic tragedy. Other dreams of servants are good. You will emerge from your current obscurity in due time and you will never again need to hobnob with *hoi polloi*. Instead, you will associate only with wealthy and influential people. But you need not be on your best behavior. These people will tolerate you only because of your enormous wealth. Feel free, therefore, to act boorish, to scratch yourself on receiving lines, and to ask for beer at State dinners.

SHEEP—French scientists have recently discovered a dream phenomenon that I like to call the Beau Peep Syndrome. A dreamer dreams that he is counting sheep in order to fall asleep and dream. The dreamer therefore pinches himself to check whether he is awake—and he then awakens. Since he is confused by the nature of his dreams, he often pinches his wife, mistress, or bed partner to ascertain that he is back in the world of reality. . . . Until the Beau Peep Syndrome reaches other shores, to dream of fat sheep is good; to dream of lean sheep is bad. In either case, they portend financial change. If you dream of shearing sheep, you will marry above your station or, in some more devious way, pull the wool over some wealthy person's eyes.

SKUNK—To dream of a skunk shows that you will have a sweaty or foul-minded companion in life. This is an ominous dream for virgins of any age or either sex.

SKYSCRAPERS—To dream of these mammoth erections has great sexual significance.

SLAVE—If a woman dreams that she is a slave, the man she has married or will marry thinks of her as a household drudge. He will seek glamour elsewhere, leaving her behind to cook casseroles, wash dishes, clean bathtubs, scrub floors, burp babies, and mow the lawn. When he dies, he will leave her nothing but unpaid bills. She will be evicted from her hovel and forced to put the children to work. . . . If a man dreams of having a slave, he should feel free to abuse his wife and treat her like a drudge. She is a glutton for punishment. . . . If a man should dream he is a slave or a woman should dream that she is a slave-owner, check carefully for symptoms of masochism in the family.

SNAIL—If you dream that you step on a snail, you will become acquainted with the lowest and most plodding sort of people in the near future. They will have evil designs upon you, but they will be too lazy to carry them out. Ignore them.

SNAKE—If you see a snake, you have a need to unwind. You are so coiled up and tense that you are driving yourself into an early grave. . . . If you kill a snake in a dream, this is good; if you merely beat the snake senseless, so much the better. Both indicate that you will vanquish your enemies—but the latter also implies that you won't go to jail for doing so. . . . Freud says the snake is "the most important" of phallic symbols.

SNOW—To the farmer, snow denotes a bumper crop, which is good for the economy. To soldiers in peacetime, however, it means that their designs will be frustrated, which is good for the rest of us. To airplane pilots and passengers alike, it denotes icing on the wings. In general, a dream of snow portends a long period of tranquility.

SOLDIERS—After a dream of soldiers, it is wise to change your name, address, and situation. Even this may not help. The consequences of this dream are often inescapable—particularly if it involves sergeants or lieutenant colonels.

SPIDER—Quoth one authoritative dream book: "You have dreamed of a spider? Lady Luck smiles upon you! Good fortune is to be yours—success in all your schemes, matrimony to crown your courtship, children to grace your marriage, prosperity to reward your labors in business. If, however, you have killed a spider in your dreams, all is reversed. Woe unto you!" . . . Quoth another: "The Spider is symbolic of industry, and also suggestive of successful cunning. It is not without purport, however, that the zoologist knows that the lady spider, once her husband has fulfilled his amative purpose, devours him. Let the male beware of the spider woman."

SQUIRREL—If a man dreams that he keeps a squirrel at home, he loves either a shrewish woman or a scheming servant. If a married woman has the same dream, she should ascertain that she—and not her chambermaid—is the shrewish woman of her husband's dreams. . . . If someone else has this dream or any other dream of squirrels, it is meaningless except as a reminder that other people have problems, too.

STAIN—If you are a woman and you dream that you or your clothes are stained, then you are pregnant and don't let anyone tell you otherwise. Freud wrote about a young mother who dreamed of milk stains on the front of her blouse. Freud called this an "indication of pregnancy. . . . The young mother hoped she would have more nourishment for the second child than she had for the first." . . . If you dream of menstruation, you are compensating for the fact that your menses will stop. Freud called this a "clever way of giving notice of . . . first pregnancy." Thus, if a woman dreams of stains, she should begin at once to knit tiny things. . . . If a man dreams of stains, he should prepare himself for impending fatherhood.

STARCH—To dream that you are starching linen means better luck to poor people; decay and disrepute to the rich. A starched collar signifies a stiff neck.

STARS—Hippocrates once wrote: "When the stars appear [in a dream] to wander this way and that with no necessity, the dream indicates disturbance of the soul due to worry." Since Hippocrates was a gifted physician as well as a dream interpreter, he also prescribed a cure for this dream: laughter and light thoughts. Today, we have television.

STATUES—To dream of statues and other graven images is to anticipate wealth. But to dream that you see brazen images moving around implies that you should cut down on your movie-going.

STRIPES—It is good to see others in stripes, whether they be in striped clothes, sergeant's stripes, prison stripes, or the stripes that result from whippings. Unfortunately, this is a most propitious dream for wife-beaters. . . . It is never good, however, to see oneself in stripes.

SUBWAY—To dream of rapid transit systems hints that you will marry beneath your station.

SUNTAN LOTION—See OIL.

SWANS—Swans are excellent birds of omen if they keep their mouths shut. If so, they will bring joy to your world. "The fruit of your loins will have beauty and health and a pervasive sanity," says an Ontario dream interpreter. If, on the other hand, a swan should sing swan songs or make other ominous noises in your dreams, you will die.

SWELLING—See WARTS.

SWIMMING—See WATER.

SWOON—If you dream that you swoon, avoid hypertension, overwork, and stuffy rooms.

T

TAXI—To dream that you are hailing a cab prefigures a bumpy journey through life. If you dream of riding in a driverless taxi, you will receive an unexpected sum of money. If there is a driver in your dream, some cabbie will receive an unexpected sum of money—which probably fell out of your pocket while you were riding in his cab.

TEETH—Most Freudian dream interpreters go on at great length about loss-of-tooth dreams. They imply that sexual repression makes us transfer dreams of masturbation to the upper parts of the body. Freud himself says: "The extraction of a tooth by another is usually to be interpreted as castration," which is commonly feared as punishment for getting caught while masturbating. (This penology is seldom practiced nowadays in enlightened societies.) Freud also notes: "Dreams of pulling teeth, and of teeth falling out, are interpreted in popular belief to mean the death of a connection. Psychoanalysis can admit of such a meaning only at the most as a joking allusion. . . ." Anna Eva Fay, however, thought otherwise. Miss Fay once declared quite humorlessly: "To dream that you lose a tooth denotes the loss of some friend by death and that troubles and misfortunes are about to attend you. To the lover, it *shews* [italics mine: *shews* was one of Miss Fay's pet affectations] the loss of his sweetheart's affection." . . . To dream that you have false teeth signifies that reports of your death will be greatly exaggerated. But if you actually possess false teeth, then your dream's meaning is obvious: Your tongue is caressing your naked gums and thereby wreaking erotic havoc. . . . To dream that you have a loose tooth hints that you have already embraced moral laxity . . . . If you dream that you grow new front teeth, brace yourself! You will have as many children as you have new teeth.

TELEVISION—Harken, dreamer! To see a television set in your dream portends that you will receive unexpected news from afar. The news may change your life, but, then again, it may not. Rest assured, however, that you have just experienced an important dream. Good night and good luck!

TOAD—"The toad," says a dream interpreter with a theological bent, "in the dream is as the Serpent in the Garden of Eden: a warning to you and to all mankind. Warnings are unpleasant but useful. The lewd toad's prophecy of your ruin can be made the lying thing it ought to be."

TRAIN—See APPOINTMENT and RIDING.

TRAVEL—See RIDING.

U

UNFAITHFUL—Always a dream of contrary. To dream that your husband, wife, or lover is unfaithful is to know for certain that nothing exists but unbending loyalty.

URINE—I quote once again from the Chester Beatty Papyrus Three of the Twelfth Egyptian Dynasty (2000-1790 B.C.): "If a man sees himself in a dream drinking his own urine, this is good. He will eat his son's own possessions." Four thousand years of Togetherness have not diluted this dream's meaning.

V

VAULTS—To dream you dwell in vaults, deep cellars, or anywhere underground implies that you will either lose a lover or else marry a divorced person. . . . Vault dreams are often taken as symbols of female genitalia —an honor that Freud also extended to small boxes, chests, cupboards, gardens, flowers, doors, bottles, ovens, cavities, ships, and gravy boats.

VELVET—If a young lady dreams that she is wearing velvet, she will have many male admirers—but not nearly so many as she would have if she wore nothing at all.

VINEGAR—To dream that you drink or bathe in vinegar is a symptom of perversion.

VIOLIN—To dream of playing the violin foretells good will between man and wife, master and servant, black and white, Jew and Gentile, friend and enemy, even cops and robbers.

VIRGIN—To talk with one of these rare creatures in a dream foretells incomparable ecstasy and intense pleasure in real life. If, however, a maiden dreams that she has been deflowered, she will soon lose that which she holds most dear. If a married woman dreams that she is a virgin, either her frigidity or her past promiscuity will be disclosed.

VOTE—If you dream of casting your ballot—be it for a cleaner New York, for Richard M. Nixon, for William Jennings Bryan, or for repealing the income tax—your affairs will not go well. For sick people, such a dream can be fatal.

W

WAR—To dream of war nowadays is good only for soldiers, munitions makers, and black marketeers. For the rest of us, such a dream signifies horrors that cannot be imagined in our wildest dreams. To a mother, it means that she will raise her boy to be a soldier. To a pacifist, it foretells police brutality. To a policeman, it means he will hate himself in the morning. . . . No matter who you are, a dream of war will result in a serious interruption to your way of life.

WARTS—To dream that you have warts, swellings, pustules, growths, or moles generally signifies that you will go away for a number of years and come home wealthy. Moles lend themselves to various interpretations, a number of which are contained in the "Signification of Moles" section of *Old Aunt Dinah's*. One important entry: "Moles on the thighs or loins of men or women are signs of want; especially being found on the left side of the body or the left side of the thigh. Let such take heed of venereal misfortunes."

WASP—See BEE.

WATER—"People who dream often, and with great enjoyment, of swimming, cleaving the waves, etc., have usually been bedwetters, and they now repeat in the dream a pleasure which they have long since learned to forego," said Freud. . . . "To dream of springs and wells denotes some disturbance of the bladder," said Hippocrates. . . . "The symbolic significance of water is mainly derived from its unconscious equivalencies . . . with uterine fluid. . . . It is probably the commonest symbol employed in birth fantasies," said Dr. Ernest Jones. . . . From *Everybody's Dream Book:* "Do you dream of clear water? Comfort and happiness will be yours. Of dirty water? Sorrow and trouble face you. Is it a gushy current? Unexpected enemies threaten you, but you will overcome them. Stagnant water presages a severe illness which may be fatal. Is the water drying up or disturbed? Your affairs will improve. Are you carrying the water without spilling it? This augurs domestic trouble. Are you *drinking* clear water? Splendid! This is a most fortunate sign." . . .

WEASEL—To dream of weasels shows that one's beloved will renege on the marriage vows. To certain men, it specifically warns that their wives see them not as husbands but as father-substitutes. The easiest way to remember this dream's punning implication is: "Pop 'Goes the Weasel." It is a dream of great subtlety, so handle it delicately.

WHALE—Except to crews of nuclear submarines, dreams of whales are good. Readers will find white whales far less elusive in dreams than in *Moby Dick*. Symbolically speaking, since whales are by far the greatest of all mammals—present company included!—the dreamer has greatness within him.

WIFE—She who dreams that she is a wife will never wed. He who dreams that he pets or pampers his wife will have marital difficulties. He who dreams that his wife is married to another will often worry about infidelity, but he does not always have cause for alarm. A dream that your wife is chasing you with a rolling pin may seem quaint, but it hints ominously that she is trying to be the man in the family. To dream that she is tongue-lashing you shows that you are henpecked.

WOUND—   "To dream of a wound is sorrow and grief;
              Of dressing a wound is cure and relief."
                  —from a turn-of-the-century rhyme.

If a young man dreams that he is wounded by a sword, he will soon take a mistress who will gratify his every whim, but never mention marriage. If, however, he mentions marriage to her, she will turn into a veritable pumpkin through the miracle of compulsive eating. . . . If a virgin dreams that she is wounded by a sword, the seemingly experienced man to whom she will give herself will turn out to be a virgin himself. . . . If a businessman dreams of a wound, his ledgers will bleed with red ink. If a soldier dreams that he is recovering from a wound, he can look forward to a Purple Heart and other honors. To lawyers and pregnant women, wound dreams denote miscarriages of justice.

X

X—There is not a single dream symbol beginning with the letter X that is worthy of mention in these pages.

Y

YOUNG—To dream that you are as young as you once were is merely wishful dreaming.

Z

ZEBRA—If you dream of zebras, you have no time for idle dreams. Be vigilant.

THE END

BIBLIOGRAPHY

Having ably bolstered the author's own experience in the field of dream interpretation, the following three dozen books and articles are gratefully acknowledged as sources of material. Those marked with an asterisk (*) are particularly recommended as supplementary reading for those who wish to delve more deeply into dreams:

*BARKER, James J.: "How Modern Psychiatrists View Your Dreams," *McCall's*, July, 1962.

CAYCE, Edgar (selections): *The Meaning and Use of Dreams;* Virginia Beach: Edgar Cayce Publishing Company, 1960.

CELLINI, Benvenuto: *The Autobiography of Benvenuto Cellini;* translated by John Addington Symonds; New York: The Modern Library (Random House).

*DIAMOND, Edwin: *The Science of Dreams;* Garden City, N.Y.: Doubleday & Company, Inc., 1962.

*DUDLEY, Geoffrey A.: *Dreams: Their Meaning and Significance;* London: Thorsons Publishers, Ltd.

*ELLIOT, John: "What Dreams Mean," *Coronet,* August, 1955.

*ELLIS, Havelock: *The World of Dreams;* Boston and New York: Houghton Mifflin Company, 1926.

FAY, Anna Eva: *Anna Eva Fay's Somnolency and Guide to Dreams;* Melrose Highlands, Mass., 1900.

FRANCIS, Leo: *Dreams and Their Meaning: 550 Dreams Explained;* London: Ward, Lock and Co., Ltd., 1958.

*FREUD, Sigmund: *The Interpretation of Dreams;* translated by Dr. A. A. Brill; New York: The Modern Library (Random House), 1950.

*FREUD, Sigmund: *On Dreams;* translated by James Strachey; New York: W. W. Norton and Co., 1952.

*FROMM, Erich: *The Forgotten Language: An In-*

troduction to the Understanding of Dreams, Fairy Tales and Myths; New York: Rinehart and Co., 1951.

*GILMAN, Leonard, M.D.: *Insomnia and its Relation to Dreams;* New York and Philadelphia: J. B. Lippincott Co., 1958.

*HAVEMANN, Ernest; "What Do Your Dreams Mean?", *McCall's,* July, 1957.

HERODOTUS: *The Persian Wars;* translated by George Rawlinson; New York: The Modern Library (Random House), 1942.

HUXLEY, Aldous: *Heaven and Hell;* New York: Harper and Bros., 1956.

KELLER, Helen: *The World I Live In;* New York: The Century Co., 1910.

*KIMMINS, C.W.: *Children's Dreams;* New York: Longmans, Green and Co., 1920.

LEADBETER, C.W.: *Dreams: What They Are and How They are Caused;* Madras, India: The Theosophical Publishing House, 1957.

LEVIN, Meyer: *In Search;* New York: Horizon Press, Inc., 1950.

MILLARD, Joseph: *Edgar Cayce: Man of Miracles;* London: Neville Spearman, Ltd., 1961.

*MURPHY, Russ: *Do You Believe in Dreams?;* Chicago: Reilly and Lee, 1950.

OMARR, Sydney: *Dream-Scope;* Hollywood: Ninth House Publishing Co., 1961.

PETERSEN, William N.: *Dreams: Our Judge and Jury;* Virginia Beach: The Edgar Cayce Publ. Co., 1951.

*RATCLIFF, A. J. J.: *A History of Dreams;* London: Grant Richards, Ltd., 1923.

*RHINE, J. B.,: "Do Dreams Come True?", *Reader's Digest,* March, 1955.

*SEROG, Max, M.D.; *New Light on Dreams*: *A New Approach to the Dream Problem;* Boston: The House of Edinboro, 1953.

*SHARPE, Ella Freeman: *Dream Analysis: A Practical Handbook in Psychoanalysis;* New York: W. W. Norton and Co., 1937.

STEVENSON, Robert Louis: *Across the Plains: with Other Memories and Essays* (including "A Chapter on Dreams"); New York: Charles Scribner's Sons, 1892.

UTTLEY, Alison: *The Stuff of Dreams;* London: Faber and Faber, Ltd., 1953.

VAN HUYT, Dirk: *Your Prophetic Dreams: With Copious References to Sacred and Profane Love;* London: Comyns, Ltd.

*WOLFF, Werner: *The Dream—Mirror of Conscience;* New York: Grune and Stratton, 1952.

Everybody's Dream Book: Your Dreams Explained; Los Angeles: Bantam Publications, 1942.

Napoleon's Book of Fate Captured at the Battle of Leipsic with Interpretation of Dreams.

Old Aunt Dinah's Policy Player's Sure Guide to Lucky Dreams and Lucky Numbers to which is added Sibyl's Book of Fate and the Complete Oraculum.

The Universal Dreamer; London: R. Walwyn.

The End

Other Distinguished Books From Pyramid

ESP

by **Susy Smith.** Ghosts, visions, telepathy, life after death—the fascinating story of the uncanny world of Extrasensory Perception. (X776—60c)

TAKE OFF YOUR MASK

by **Ludwig Eidelberg, M.D.** This book has been written to give you an opportunity to "listen in" on a psychoanalyst's working day and to understand the emotional problems of his patients. (G558—35c)

MENTAL HOSPITAL

by **Morton M. Hunt.** Brings you face to face with the fascinating effective new methods which medical science employs to achieve its remarkable recoveries for the mentally disturbed. (F762—50c)

YOGA FOR PERFECT HEALTH

by **Alain.** A system of health and hygiene of body and mind that can help give you a vigorous and happy life. Contains photographs demonstrating the main Yoga postures. (X659—60c)

13 FAMOUS PATIENTS

by **Noah D. Fabricant, M.D.** Amazing medical facts and ease histories of famous personalities such as Roosevelt, Hitler, Gandi, Freud, Gauguin and Gershwin. (R649—50c)

I CRIED IN THE DARK

by **Ann Scott.** The deeply personal story of a woman who reconstructed her life through psychoanalysis and saved her marriage from the despair of frigidity. (G371—35c)

ENTIRE SELECTION ONLY $2.50, POSTAGE PAID

(for single copies add 10c to list price to cover postage and handling)

PYRAMID BOOKS, Dept. R799, 444 Madison Avenue, New York 22, N.Y.

Please send me the following books at the special price of 6 books for $2.50, postage paid (single copies add 10c to list price to cover postage and handling.)

X776   G558   R762   X659   R649   G371

Name _____

Address _____

City _____ State _____